THE POWER OF MATURITY

THE
Power
OF
Maturity

BY

LOUIS BINSTOCK

HAWTHORN BOOKS, INC.
PUBLISHERS NEW YORK
W. Clement Stone, President

To our sons,
Dr. William A. Binstock
and
Dr. Robert H. Binstock

ACKNOWLEDGMENTS

Passage from *Your First Year of Marriage* by Tom McGinnis. Used by permission of Doubleday & Company, Inc.

Paragraph from "The psychiatric fad these days is identity. . . ." by Russell Baker, © 1968 by The New York Times Company. Reprinted by permission.

Paragraph from critic's review of "More Stately Mansions" © 1967 by The New York Times Company. Reprinted by permission.

Quotation from *Markings* by Dag Hammarskjöld, © 1964 by Alfred A. Knopf, Inc. Reprinted by permission.

Quotation from *Dag Hammarskjöld* by Sven Stolpe. Used by permission of Charles Scribner's Sons.

Material from *The Road to Successful Living* by Louis Binstock, © 1958 by Simon and Schuster, Inc. Reprinted by permission.

Material from *Peace of Mind* by Joshua Loth Liebman, © 1946 by Simon and Schuster, Inc. Reprinted by permission.

Material from *The Chosen* by Chaim Potok, © 1967 by Simon and Schuster, Inc. Reprinted by permission.

Excerpts from "The Hairy Ape," by Eugene O'Neill, © 1922 and renewed 1950 by Eugene O'Neill. Courtesy of Random House, Inc.

Excerpts from *What Men Live By* by Richard Cabot. Courtesy of Houghton Mifflin Company.

Material from *Man Against Himself* by Karl Menninger, © 1956 by Harcourt, Brace & World, Inc. Reprinted by permission.

A general statement of the eight criteria of emotional maturity from *Emotional Maturity* by Dr. Leon J. Saul, published by J. B. Lippincott Company.

Quotation from *Death Be Not Proud* by John Gunther. Used by permission of Harper & Row, Publishers.

Quotation from *The Temper of Our Time* by Eric Hoffer. Used by permission of Harper & Row, Publishers.

Quotation from *Journal of a Soul* by Pope John XXIII, © 1965 by Geoffrey Chapman, Ltd. Used by permission of McGraw-Hill Book Company.

Material from *How to Recruit, Select and Place Salesmen* by Dr. Robert N. McMurry. Courtesy of The Dartnell Press.

CONTENTS

THE POWER OF MATURITY

Chapter One

WHAT IS MATURITY?

We will begin with two stories.

The first is from a Gypsy folk tale. It concerns two men who are brushing their horses and talking quietly to each other. One man says to his friend, "Do you know the ancient wisdom of our people?"

"As much as it is given me to know."

"Then tell me; which is the greater, the oak or the dandelion?"

The second man is tempted to answer that the oak is greater. Surely it is taller, stronger, and more useful than the dandelion. But he suspects a trap. He replies, "The dandelion."

His friend tells him, however, that neither the huge oak nor the tiny dandelion is to be considered greater than the other. Old Romany lore points out that greatness consists in *the potential of one's particular self*. Has the dandelion grown into a fully matured, healthy, and beautiful flower? Then it is greater—far greater—than a stunted oak.

The second story comes out of a vastly different background.

In the early nineteenth century, in the small village of Hanipol, in eastern Europe, there lived a great teacher named Zusya. He was a leader of a Jewish sect, the Hasidim, which chose the mystical rather than the rational approach to God. Attempting to solve the divine mystery, they searched for the formula for the ideal man. Thus they might be able to follow the Biblical commandment: "Ye shall be perfect even as I, the Lord your God, am perfect."

Zusya had chosen as his model the great Moses, God's most trusted servant. But after many years of profound study and community service, Zusya felt he was still as far below the peak of Moses' towering character as was the village of Hanipol below the peaks of the surrounding mountains.

One night, exhausted, he fell asleep, and God appeared to him in a dream. "Why are you so disturbed, my son?" asked God. "You have climbed high on the ladder of perfection."

Awed, Zusya whispered, "But my days on earth will soon be ended, and I must climb so much higher to make myself like Moses."

Smiling, God answered, "Worry no more. When you appear before my throne of judgment, I will not ask, 'Why were you not like Moses?' I will ask, 'Why were you not Zusya, your best possible self?' You are not expected to reach the perfection of Moses. You are expected to fulfill the fullest potential of Zusya, yourself."

And so the men of the field and forest and the men of the Torah had come to the same conclusion: one's own greatness lies in fulfilling one's best self.

This is maturity—a process that ends only with death. In man or in plant it is a continual growing. Yes, as the dandelion seed fulfills itself by becoming a mature dandelion, so should a man ask, not to become another Moses or Jesus or Buddha or Einstein or Schweitzer, but to grow until he is his best *self*. And, invariably, when a man knows he is fulfilling his own particular seed of growth, he finds he has far more strength and ability and courage than he had ever realized he possessed. What happens then? He should continue to grow and find even more.

Maturity is not a state of being; it is a state of becoming. You may say of yourself: "I am not a human *being*; I am a human *becoming*." This play on words forms a memorable pointer toward the best in life.

Now take this concept of personal fulfillment and apply it in as down-to-earth a manner as you wish. You will see endless possibilities for success and joy. The mature person directs himself toward success in his education, success in his marriage, and success in helping his children find their own maturity. The mature person is qualified to take life as it comes and handle it well. Of course, he has no guarantee that he will always be happy, or always be free of pain, emotional or physical. Yet, no matter what happens, he has in his maturity the means of finding the good, the true, and the beautiful. He has the gift of living a life that is truly complete.

The word "maturity" is comparatively new. Even Freud, the father of psychoanalysis, never used it. But the concept is old. In the world of antiquity, wise men saw the difference between mere *learning*, the acquiring of facts, and *wisdom*, an innate quality. What the ancients called "wisdom" is, in many ways, what we mean by "maturity." One may also call maturity the ability to discern the difference between that which is good and that which is bad—not only in the moral sense, but also in the practical sense, of being able to discern what in the long run is good or bad to live with and for. Morally speaking, this must also include the consideration of what is good or bad for your fellow men. In theological terms this means determining that which is God's and that which is Satan's. In psychological terms it is that which concretely helps your person and that which concretely harms it. In sociological terms it is that which helps you help others establish a stable and peaceful community, and that which creates the social conflicts that result in strife and violence and war.

The more we deal with all the various aspects of maturity, however, the more we realize that maturity is the inheritance of every human being. Not all of us find our maturity. In all of us, however, there lies the seed, prepared to unfold, develop, and *become* as we reach different stages of growth with our advancing years.

The miracle of birth is in itself the first stage. The seed that was planted in favorable fertile soil has, after nine months of proper nourishment and care, ripened into a viable human being. Listen carefully to the newborn infant's cry. Watch its twisting head and its wriggling little body; its flailing arms and legs. Look into its eyes, trying to focus. There, in every aspect, are the beginnings of maturity—so tiny as to be almost imperceptible, but there nevertheless.

See maturity, if you will, as your control center—a panel of dials and instruments from which you manage your life. Your maturity serves you now as a shock absorber, now as a thermostat, now as a leveler or stabilizer. It continually influences your thoughts, your emotions, and even your soul, the searchlight of your aspirations. Your maturity acts as your computer; it combines, analyzes, and evaluates all the data that pour in upon you through your senses. Your maturity is *not* your I.Q. A person of modest I.Q. but real maturity can get more life-success than can a genius lacking in maturity.

I recall a highly successful, brilliant man of fifty who one day telephoned me for an immediate appointment. I could tell by his voice that he was desperate but, even so, his appearance when he arrived shocked me.

With nervous hands and trembling words he unfolded his story. He had thought he had "a little eye trouble." Now, after having visited the most qualified specialists, he knew he had both cataracts and glaucoma. He was broken, floored, ruined, destroyed. He couldn't face what was happening to him.

I told him he was very lucky. Although he was ready to explode at such a statement, I calmed him down by reminding him that only within the past ten years or so had the means been found to arrest glaucoma. It was 1967, not 1957. The excess pressure within his eyes could be held at a tolerable level. He knew, too, that cataracts can now be removed easily and safely. Not only would his sight be preserved, but, in the end, he might see better than ever.

He sighed. "Yes, that is what the doctors told me," he said, passing his hands wearily across his eyes. "But I just can't help worrying."

"You wouldn't be normal if you were not worried," I said. "It's a great shock to be told you have serious eye ailments. Naturally, at first you fear you're going blind."

He seemed to be a bit comforted. "You mean it's normal to get so upset?"

"Perhaps not everyone would get quite that upset, but it's still normal. Well now, think a bit further. You have afflictions, but think of the afflictions you might have had. Suppose you had had a paralytic stroke. You might be doomed to spend the rest of your life in bed. Or suppose you had been told you have a fatal cancer. Then to all your other troubles would be added the knowledge that your doctors could not help you. But you have been told that your doctors can help you and they will help you. Have you looked at your situation that way? You have great problems, but the experts, the doctors, have assured you that they know how to solve those problems, and they will. Why, that's great news! In a little while you are going to see clearly and easily once more, and you'll be able to go on with your life that was running so well."

I did not mention the word "maturity." I was telling him indirectly, however, to summon aid from his core of maturity—and he did. In a little while his entire manner underwent a transformation. His shock absorber of maturity cushioned the blow. His leveler put his emotions back on an even keel. His thermostat reduced his high fever of worry to a fairly normal emotional temperature. When he left, he thanked me and he even summoned up a smile.

I knew that he would worry again, but that now he'd put a reasonable limit on his worry. A day would come when all his apprehension would be only a fading memory. And he'd know how his maturity had helped carry him through. I saw him not long ago. He looks better, younger, and happier than he has looked in years.

This is a story with a happy ending. For many, however, there is no recovery from some blighting injury or illness. Yet sometimes among the most severely stricken we still find real happiness, on another level, seized out of the ashes by the force of maturity and made warm and alive again.

I was visiting my wife's sister in a small resort village when she introduced me to her most admired and cherished friend. He lived in a wheelchair. In his teens he had been stricken with a disease that left almost his entire body paralyzed. He could not walk—nor even crawl, for he could not raise his arms. Yet his maturity, never paralyzed, reminded him that his eyes could see, his ears could hear, his lips could speak, and his hands at least could move.

So he learned the art of printing. He set up a small printing shop in one bedroom of the little house where he lived with his widowed mother. His telephone brought in orders. His hands were able to fill the orders. For more than twenty-five years he had run this business, and his income was more than enough to take care of the household's needs.

This was remarkable enough, but even more remarkable was his spirit. After only five or ten minutes of conversation, you realized you were in the presence of a very mature man. You forgot his handicaps. You knew only the cheerfulness of his manner, the smile on his face, the sweetness of his voice, and the breadth and depth of his many interests in life. For this man in a wheelchair *lived*. He had mined deep into his core of maturity and he had come up with a great treasure. He enjoyed life as fully as any normally active person I have ever met—and he could give good instruction to many who let mere trifles sour their existence.

Maturity, like a precious gem, has many facets—many directions from which it sheds its beams upon our lives. Later we shall set forth many particularized definitions of maturity. You can see already, however, how many volumes we speak when we say, "*Maturity is not a state of being; it is a state of becoming.*" To complete the frame in which to hold this entire general concept of maturity, we may now add: "*Maturity is to be found in dealing wisely with the phenomena of existence.*" Throughout this book, there will be many reminders of these major maturity themes.

It is significant that man has been endowed with a longer period of infancy and childhood than any other animal. Yet he is far more complex than any other creature. As Shakespeare said: "What a piece of work is man!" Man seems to need the extra time he takes to grow into an adult—not only physically, but mentally, emotionally, and spiritually as well. Strongly affected by his times and by his immediate surroundings, he may take a greater or a lesser time in which to grow out of childhood. He may as a child show maturity "beyond his years," or, like Alice in Wonderland, he may have to run very hard in order merely to stay in the same maturity-place.

When you are conscious of maturity, however, you can feel it growing within yourself. You can summon it; and tell it to perform services for you. Yet for most people it does not come all at once. Especially after decades of acting like a large child, you may have to take yourself well in hand before you can find, nourish, and bring forth your maturity.

Even as growth itself takes time, so does it take time to develop mature attitudes toward life. "No great thing is created suddenly," Epictetus teaches, "any more than is a bunch of grapes or a fig. If you tell me you desire a fig, I answer you this: There must be time. Let it first blossom, then bear fruit, then ripen. Since then the fruit of a fig tree is not brought to perfection suddenly or in one hour—do you think to possess instantaneously the fruit of the human mind? I warn you to expect it not." And so it is with the core of maturity. You must give it time to grow and develop. Know, however, that this precious seed is denied to nobody. Even with a retarded child, it is always there.

There is very little you can do for your maturity during the first stage of life, infancy. During that period, the maturity of your caretakers—parents, friends, the family physician, or older siblings—helps in forming you. However, at the second stage of life (which begins at about seven years of age), your own maturity begins to show itself, sometimes with surprising strength.

In the third stage of life (which begins at about the age of fourteen), you are competent to take almost complete charge, and, in earlier days, when people died much younger than they do today, you might have begun to consider yourself an adult. In the fourth stage, being over twenty-one and enriched with education, you are quite capable of applying your maturity to a considerable portfolio of problems. At forty or so, as you enter upon the fifth stage of life, you have had considerable education (including informal education) and experience, and you should have a good grip upon your affairs. At sixty, where you begin the sixth stage of the journey of the years, you are gathering in many fruits of your long planting and tending; you should have a clear vision of the final part of the journey, too, and you can plan for it with assurance. And at the last stage—say, when you are past seventy-five years of age—you still are growing, becoming! But you know how to bring your earthly voyage to a successful, peaceful conclusion, for, with maturity, you made it good all the way.

We are talking, however, of *human* maturity. The creature who calls himself Man is too complex to be entirely consistent. So, in examining this maturity that everyone praises, this maturity that can do so much toward helping us conquer life's problems, a puzzled reader well may say, "How can you depend on it? How do you even know it when you see it?"

Again, someone has observed, "Often I think that the entire concept of maturity is just a fraud; that there are no people over fourteen, only long-term children buried in wrinkles and pomposity. I think that I myself am only a makeshift adult with stilts inside my long pants and manhood painted on my face; and that suddenly these trappings will drop away and expose the little fellow underneath with his finger in his mouth. Still, there are times when I do feel really grown up; but it is as though it just happened —as though I had just experienced some singular Bar Mitzvah, attained some thundering new majority attained so far by no one else."

Yes, that is the way it often goes—quite inconsistently! Expect the inconsistency, and it won't bother you. At the age of thirteen, a Jewish boy is Bar Mitzvahed—traditionally and theoretically he becomes a member of the congregation, and, in that sense at least, is supposed to assume the duties of a man. Yet when does the truly effective Bar Mitzvah occur? When comes the maturity of which St. Paul spoke so vividly when he said, "When I was a child I spake as a child, I felt as a child, I thought as a child; now that I am become a man I have put away childish things"? You will have to see for yourself. You will have to see *in* yourself.

You may be mature in running your business, but a child when it comes to "putting away for a rainy day." You may be mature while you work but give way to petulant childishness on the golf course or at the card table. I know successful businessmen who are just like that. I know active, civic-minded women who spark charities and other worthy functions but cannot find harmony with their own husbands and children. And in marriage one may be mature in all areas save that of sex, or money, or in the simple friendship that is missing in so many unions.

You can notice in yourself and in others that childish behavior is often the result of some sudden emotional strain or friction. A person of strong maturity will not be seriously bothered; but if your own maturity does slip there is always a next time in which to do better. Did you say something really stupid when someone annoyed you at a dinner party? Did you act stingily on some occasion, and later wish you had been more generous? Were you crude in your manner so that you hurt someone whom you did not wish to hurt? Have you had a lapse in morals, and do you berate yourself and find it hard to live with your guilt? It happens. But it need not go on forever. The more mature you make yourself, the more proof you become against such lapses. You seem to develop a strong instinct for doing and saying the right thing at the right time—an instinct that is naturally an invaluable aid in the search for success, love, and happiness.

Now and again you may get a great boost toward maturity from some teacher who understands it. Such a teacher may be a psychologist, a psychiatrist, a wise friend, a priest, a minister, or a rabbi. In the last analysis, however, it is up to you. You must want to be mature. You must be willing to do something toward attaining, at any age, your own full-fledged new "Bar Mitzvah"—your great burgeoning of maturity.

The sages of the Talmud declared that every child of God is molded out of a distinct and different die. Each of us is stamped with our own uniqueness. No two individuals, not even identical twins, look and act exactly the same. It can be shown easily that neither are twins quite alike mentally, emotionally, morally, or spiritually. They can be born into the same family circle, reared within the same group structure during their infancy and childhood, given the same schools and the same teachers, and play with the same playmates, but they will be in many ways different individuals. And so too will their levels of maturity be different.

It seems that each of us is born with a core, or essential seed,

that is as unique as the whorls on the pads of one's fingers. Think
of this as your core of maturity. In a very broad sense, because it
is so unique and so strongly yours, it makes you what you are.

We still write much of the story in our own Book of Fate. Ultimate maturity, though never complete (because you never stop
becoming), is the joint product of the inheritance within your core
and the impact of your life-environment upon it. Your life-environment contains not only its many physical aspects but also the environment you create within your own fund of intelligence and
emotions. You yourself control and direct a vast proportion of your
total environment. As the Bible puts it, it is for you to choose
either the blessing or the curse. Or, as it says elsewhere: "As a man
thinketh in his heart, so is he."

By and large, therefore, this is a do-it-yourself book. It cannot
take the place of a psychiatrist or other professional help if that is
what you need. It can, however, teach almost anyone how to believe and behave maturely in most instances and most of the time
—so that he does grow in his inward stature and does deal wisely,
as a rule, with the phenomena of his existence.

This book is carefully planned so that, when you have finished
reading it (and thinking about it) you should be able to spot your
own immaturities and either remove them or render them harmless. You will discover in these pages a code of guidance for your
personal welfare, success, happiness, and peace of mind. You will
discover keys to love and domestic joy. And you will understand
maturity and use it as the great gift it is, to help you constantly as
you move from where you are to the pinnacle of success and good
living, which is where you want to be and where you ought to be.

Let us have one more story before we proceed. It is a favorite
story that illustrates the power of maturity, it is a true story and a
great story.[1]

About two hundred years ago, the Jewish philosopher Moses
Mendelssohn visited Hamburg. There he made the acquaintance
of the rich aristocratic merchant Guggenheim.

Mendelssohn was a hunchback. But his hump seemed to bother

---

[1] Theodor Reik, *Of Love and Lust* (New York: Grove Press), 1967.

him less than many an invisible "hump" of bitterness or inferiority bothers other men. Yet, when he met Guggenheim's charming daughter, Frumtje, and when he fell in love with her, and when he saw some answering gleam in her tender eyes—surely then he could not have been unaware of his own physical unattractiveness.

After a stay of several weeks, he was ready to leave Hamburg. Now he made his move. He called upon Guggenheim and forthrightly asked if he might bring up the subject of marriage to the rich and powerful man's daughter.

The merchant hesitated for a significantly long time. Mendelssohn asked him to say frankly what was on his mind.

"Well," said Guggenheim at last, "you are known far and wide as a very wise man. I believe you are a good man. And yet—and yet—I must tell you that my child was a bit frightened when she first saw you. Because—because—"

"Because I am a hunchback?"

Sadly, the father nodded. That was it.

The young and very mature philosopher expressed no surprise. He asked only for the privilege of seeing Frumtje alone so that he might say farewell to her. Admitted to her room, he found her busy with needlework. He spoke of various matters. Carefully and gradually, he led around to the subject that was nearest his heart. At last he asked her, "Do you believe that marriages are made in heaven?"

She looked up, flushed, and looked down again. "I have learned this." The flying needle paused. "Yes, Mr. Mendelssohn. Yes, I believe it."

"It is so," he said gently. "Now let me tell you about something strange that happened when I was born. As you know, at a child's birth, according to our Jewish tradition, they call out in heaven that the birth has occurred. And when it is a boy, they announce, 'Such-and-such boy will have this-and-that girl for a wife.'

"Well, there I was, just born, and I heard the name of my future wife announced. At the same time, I heard the great far-off Voice say, 'Unfortunately, the poor little girl, Frumtje, will have a terrible hump on her back.' Quick as a flash, I cried out, 'O Lord God, if a girl is hunch-backed she will grow up bitter and hard.

Please, O Lord, give her hump to me and let Frumtje develop into a well-formed, lovely, and charming young lady.' "

Mendelssohn waited. Slowly, Frumtje looked up again. She dropped her needlework, rose, and approached him with her hands outstretched. And so these two mature young people bridged chasms that would have defeated the immature; great gulfs of physical deformity and revulsion—and also the gulf of wealth, for Mendelssohn had only modest dreams. Yet she became his faithful, loving wife and he her grateful, adoring husband.

To see the difference between passing pleasure and lasting worth —that is maturity. To sense the importance of looking beyond any surface appearance and searching out the true substance of a thing or a man or a circumstance—that is maturity. It applies in marriage, it applies in making one's livelihood, it applies in all our dealings with ourselves and with our fellow men.

Now we will go on to see what maturity is *not*—because sometimes we can be misled by a mere *appearance* of maturity.

Chapter Two

WHAT MATURITY
IS NOT

In *The Man Who Laughed*, Victor Hugo tells of a traveling circus that presented some tiny midgets as its special attraction. These midgets had been artificially produced. While in their infancy, they had been encased in jars the height of a three-year-old child. One may shudder at the knowledge, but they were kept in those jars throughout all the years of their normal physical growth.

In their twenties, these physically stunted creatures were released. They stood no more than three feet high and were about two feet in diameter. Yet they had been trained, while in those jars, for a life spent as entertainers. Mentally they were quite mature. After a few years of experience in the world outside their jar-prisons, they were quite at home with that world. They knew they were not normal people yet they felt normal. To the audiences at the circus, however, it was endlessly amazing to see these roly-poly little creatures talk and act like adults.

Does maturity have anything to do with one's size? No. Does maturity have anything to do with one's age? Only in a relative way. A child of seven can be far wiser than his years, while an adult of seventy may have spent all his years being very childish.

What is it that makes for maturity in a boy—say a boy at the age of eleven? I knew a boy who was sunny and pleasant, a great baseball player, sometimes an indifferent scholar—and very mature. Let me tell you how he handled a certain situation.

He came home from his last day of the school term, his report card in hand. "Dad," he said to his father, "I want to ask you something. You see, I passed in everything. Now, my friend George's father said he would give George a fielder's glove for passing, and George passed. So he is getting a fielder's glove, and —well, can I have one?"

While the father was pleased to hear that his son was doing better in school, he nevertheless shook his head regretfully. "Freddie," he said, "I am glad you passed and I congratulate you. But I don't see that you have a reward coming just for getting passing grades. What George's father does is his business. I won't reward you just for doing what is expected of you."

This showed maturity in the father, too. It is mature to stick to one's own standards when you know they are fair and just.

But we are interested in the boy. He now faced his father with a growing grin. "Okay," he said. "But suppose my passing grades were such good grades that I wasn't just promoted—I got *skipped?*" He handed his father the card that showed he had indeed been skipped an entire grade because his marks were so far above the average.

His father grinned back understandingly. "Let's go! We're going downtown to get you the best fielder's glove on the market!"

Wisdom is often equated with age. It is true that you do have to live a certain number of years or decades in order to gather a good store of life-experience; but that is not the same as maturity. Still, inevitably, the child comes to consider his father and mother, his grown-up uncles and aunts, as "wise" because they are older. So it is with gray-haired, respected, teachers, judges, and officials. Remember that the elderly *may* be mature—or they may not!

Look in the Bible and other religious writings and you will find that God's prophets are often portrayed as being comparatively young. We have no reason to believe that Amos, Hosea or Jeremiah, among others, lived to be much older than their early thirties.

We still speak of aged people who go senile as "entering their second childhood." This is a slander upon childhood. Often the child, or at least the young person, shows qualities that are lost or stifled later. Eric Hoffer, in his *The Temper of the Time*, expresses the opinion that "history is made by men who have the restlessness, impressionability, credibility, capacity for make-believe, ruthlessness and righteousness of children."

Mr. Hoffer also asserts that we can hardly know how things happened in history unless we keep in mind that, much of the time, it was juveniles who made those events happen! He reminds us that until relatively recent times man's life, judged by today's standards, was short. An excavation in one of the world's oldest cemeteries brought up skeletons that indicate that the people of the region died, on the average, at about twenty-five. And there was no evidence that the area was unusually unhealthful. This is one reason why old people (who might not have been older than fifty) were sometimes regarded as especially blessed by God and therefore possessed of great wisdom. (But in the Middle Ages and in other periods, including the present one, older people tended to be scorned and ignored.)

Mr. Hoffer also points out that the armor of fighting men preserved from the Middle Ages is often remarkably small. People were shorter in those day than they are now, but the reason for the surprising smallness of that armor is that it was worn by young men who were still growing. "They were married at 13; were warriors and leaders in their teens; and senile at 35 or 40. It is significant that the Black Prince was 16 when he won fame at the Battle of Crecy. Joan of Arc was 17 when she took Orleans from the English. . . . Montaigne tells us that he hardly ever met a man as old as 50. . . . When the dramatists [in Spain's great age, from 1550 to 1650] designated a man as old, they meant him to be about 40, yellowed, wrinkled-faced and toothless." Alexander the Great was in his early thirties when he sighed that he had no more worlds to conquer. Napoleon was still in his thirties when he became Emperor of France and almost master of all Europe. The fathers of our own American Revolution were in their twenties and thirties when they led the bold break from England.

Age is not maturity; maturity is not age. And often, how well the children know it! There is a great slice of reality in Christopher Morley's book *Thunder on the Left*, as regards a boy named Martin. One night, instead of going to bed, Martin stays up and peeps into the parlor where his parents are entertaining their friends. The boy listens awhile and wonders at how silly can they be.

What is it that seems to hold some adults in a state of perpetual childishness? Generally it is their own attitudes; they make no effort to mature. Without being nurtured, the seed or core of maturity can become arrested, like a stunted oak. You may be quite free to walk about, have fun, and do this and that; yet you have encased yourself in an invisible jar-prison the size of your teenage or even earlier, maturity.

Sometimes the process of wilful stunting—refusal to *become*—is used as an obvious means of avoiding the recognition of an unpleasant reality. I am thinking now of that sad woman in Dickens's *Great Expectations*, who, on her wedding day, was deserted at the altar. For many years afterward, she wore her wedding gown and kept herself in seclusion. Surely the refusal to become anything except a wronged woman is a complete denial of growth, fulfillment, and maturity. And yet the pose was comfortable in its way!

This case is obvious. Most often it is not so obvious when we stop growing and merely coast along.

What about I.Q.—that much-debated Intelligence Quotient we mentioned before. Can a high I.Q. be equated with a high level of maturity?

Not at all. Sometimes a high I.Q. signals a very one-sided person —a genius who is very good at his specialty but is not much good at being a human being. Often a person of high I.Q. will resentfully shirk some small but necessary task because he thinks it is "beneath him." To see the dignity of *any* honest work, or a service to another, is to show a sure sign of maturity.

As a counselor, I meet a good many confused and troubled individuals. Definitely these people have not developed their maturity; and yet, by "I.Q." standards, they may be very bright. Cruel husbands and mean wives, bent on destroying each other, often are possessed of high intelligence. Sometimes the most intelligent parents are so immature that they are actually quite stupid when it comes to handling their own children. Then why do so many immature men and women attain positions of trust and power in our communities? Because they are mature when dealing with other people's problems, and will work pathetically hard at doing so, while all the while their own personal problems remain unsolved.

Some of the world's most heartless, brutal criminals, young and old, have been persons of extraordinary intellect. They are so smart that they almost succeed in committing the perfect crimes—the crime that cannot possibly be traced to them. Read Dostoevsky's *Crime and Punishment* to see how it demands a very mature detective to gradually break down such a person.

In our own time we have had a horrible crime committed by two very intelligent young men, Loeb and Leopold, who killed little Bobby Frank.

At least, one of the pair, Leopold, the more brilliant of the two, has lived to find a true maturity. At the time of the murder, Leopold, nineteen years of age, was recognized by his teachers and classmates as a super-brain. Possessed of great unrealized potential, he had to spend thirty years in prison. I met him, a quiet man in his late forties, just before his release. We talked at length about his heinous crime. He did not offer a word of explanation or excuse. I asked him to try to recall the motivation for the crime. Did he and Loeb murder the child "for kicks"? Had they given in to a lust to kill? Leopold only shook his head in despair. The deed he had done was utterly incomprehensible to him. In fact, it was clear that this man of forty-nine was an almost entirely different person from the youth he had been at nineteen.

It was in prison that Leopold had at last matured. He did not sulk in his cell. Instead of being sorry for himself, he looked inward and started a course of self-rehabilitation. He also turned his thoughts to his fellow-prisoners, many of whom were hampered by lack of education. He initiated a prison school in which hundreds have by now completed a high school education. He himself studied a number of subjects, particularly foreign languages. That prepared him to teach. He became an X-ray expert. Meanwhile he volunteered as a human guinea pig in the testing of serums for certain deadly diseases. Facing death, he still wanted to live as a free man only to be able to pay the debt he owed society.

I am proud to say that I played a role in winning a pardon for this transformed man and in the writing of his book, *Life and Ninety-nine Years*. He is now living in Puerto Rico. He has effaced himself and his work, but I know he is one of the most useful people on the island.

We mentioned the difference between learning and wisdom. Watch for it and you will see it. Also you will find the matter touched upon over and over in history, literature, and folk wisdom of all kinds.

For example, there is an old tale about a rabbinical student at a seminary who studied hard for many years and at last came before the examining committee for his final interview before ordination. The committee asked him difficult questions about the Bible; he knew all the answers. They asked him tricky questions about the Talmud; he knew all the answers. They asked him complex questions about Jewish law and lore and the many regulations that govern orthodox Jewish life; and still he had the right answer every time.

At the end of two hours of gruelling quizzing, everyone was silent. "Have I passed?" asked the aspirant, quite sure he had passed with flying colors.

"No," said the spokesman for the committee.

"But I knew the answer to every question!"

"You did. And you only revealed that you understand it all in your head but not in your heart."

In my own experience I recall one of my seminary teachers who was a veritable storehouse of knowledge. To this day, that man's feats of memory seem incredible. We students relied upon him to brief us in general history, on the civilization of any time, on the life of any historical figure. But would we have gone to him with some personal problem that required real wisdom, judgment, *maturity* with which to find the answer? No. He was too naive to be mature in judgment. His education was large; his understanding small.

So we see that education, as well as I.Q., also fails as a measure of a man's maturity. Now and again we find a general public recognition of this ancient fact. Perhaps the long-standing public distrust of the "egghead"—however useful he may be in our so-ciety—stems from the fact that so many non-eggheads are never-theless mature, interesting, dependable people. Note too the spate of "how-to" books that has appeared in bookstores during the last two decades. They have been eagerly read, and some, such as *How to Win Friends and Influence People, The Power of Positive Thinking,* and *Peace of Mind* have enjoyed a special appeal. Now, these are not books of knowledge, data, or information. They are books of guidance and inspiration. They point out wise ways of believing and behaving, and mature approaches to achieving and associating in our complex society.

Education is a treasure, but by itself it is not an index of ma-turity. Beyond education lies the wisdom of maturity—the deep life-wisdom, felt "in the heart," that, when it is present, shows itself in everything we do.

Now comes the question of experience. How does experience equate with maturity?

Certainly we have reason to value experience, and we are con-tinually asking for experience or stressing its great worth. The father says to his son, "Now that you're out of business college, all you need is a few years of experience in real business. Then I can retire and you can take over." The physician or lawyer or clergyman with a fresh diploma is often reminded; "Now all you need is some experience." In fact, interneships and residencies are wisely required of the fledgling physician, diploma or no; and simi-lar interneships are being urged for the practice of law and for the ministry.

We recognize that in the making of a good craftsman of any kind there are not only the head, the heart, and the spirit to be considered; there is also the hand. That is, it is in the *doing* of the thing that we add the final touch to all the learning and feeling and desiring and dreaming.

John Dewey, a generation ago, insisted on "learning by doing." It was not enough to present theorems and theories or ideas and ideals in a classroom. It was equally necessary to test those ideas and prove them in the outside world. Thus, experience has become the capstone of education. While the old saying, "Experience is the best teacher," may be outworn, we do agree that experience can be, sometimes, an indispensable teacher.

We tend, then, to value experience, to trust experience, and, often, to demand experience in a man before we will engage him to deal with our health, our souls, or our fortunes. What we are really looking for, however, is maturity—that ability to handle situations, that gift of dealing wisely with the phenomena of existence—which marks the really competent man.

Look with open eyes and you will see how many persons with little or even no experience come forth with expert performances in every field. What about the young athletes in football or baseball who move right from the college stadium—or even from the high school field—into professional stardom? What about the young artists, singers, musicians, painters, sculptors, actors, writers, or poets who are so very good? They will improve—they will continue in a state of becoming—but even without experience they are ready-made "pros."

Valuable as experience is, we still must see that there can be great success with little experience. There can be maturity, and all the phenomena of maturity, with very little experience. Inside the man there is something that from the very first, it seems, has burgeoned and blossomed. Experience will help his core of maturity to grow and grow; but it will not give the original potential. So let us set aside experience as an absolute measure of maturity. Experience is good, but it is another of those human acquisitions which maturity is not.

Well then, is sophistication the same as maturity? Are sophisticated people mature people? Here we have a sad mixup. Notice how many times books and movies and plays are advertised as being "for mature people only." Here we are expected to take the meaning of "mature" as "sophisticated," and we are expected to stretch the point even farther and to see that what the advertiser really means is "for adults only." Sometimes he says so, which at least is straight talk—but that hardly solves the question of *maturity*.

Here is more confusion. In a syndicated column I read recently;

> Not only prudes and bluenoses are concerned with the problem of racy movies shown at early hours on television . . . the rather precise "Bible" of show business, *Variety*, currently has this to say, in part: "Having avoided sexual explicitness in their programs all these years, the networks find themselves submitting to a creeping maturity in their competition for the late vintage theatrical film hits. The question is—how far can they go—and how fast?"

A creeping *maturity?* Again they equate maturity with sophistication, and sophistication with adulthood. In some societies, children grow up in the midst of completely frank sex exposure and it never occurs to anybody that there should be any mystery about sex. This is not the way we order our own civilization. Still, the age of sex knowledge (if not of entire sophistication) has been creeping steadily downward.

In that highly successful play of some years ago, *Life with Father*, the father takes his son into a room to be alone with him while he explains the facts of life. Father, although a man of much experience and considerable dignity, fumbles the job and tells the boy nothing. It is a delightful scene nonetheless, but now old-fashioned. Today's child of nine or ten is quite likely to tell Pop that of course he knows all that—what else is new?

I have not observed that children are harmed by learning about sex at an earlier age than their parents did. It is not our children who are likely to engage in illicit sex activities or in the crime of rape. Primarily it is young adults who cause the trouble, but older adults—"fully matured adults" we might say quite mistakenly—cause their share of trouble with sex.

Of course, there is truth in the belief that adults will not be adversely affected by sex scenes, whereas children may be. The adult *is* generally ahead of the child in sophistication and in the actual sexual experience that enables him the better to evaluate sex. These matters are not the same as maturity—but they are something.

Watch, however, and you will note that truly mature adults are not particularly attracted by sexual display of any kind. To the mature, sex is part of life but not the greatest part; and sophistication in sex is no more valuable than any other kind of sophistication.

It is those who insist most strongly that they have been liberated from the archaic mandates of morality and religion—those who must have you know they are sophisticated and, of course, mature—who are most likely to remain in the young adolescence of maturity, especially where sex is concerned. For them, to be stimulated by sex scenes and to have their pornographic curiosity titillated again and again is still a compulsive inner need. Sometimes it is a sad attempt to recapture vanished years; the truly mature person takes his years as they come and keeps pace with them.

I repeat: sex, to the mature, is part of life; and, therefore, some interest in sex, at any age, is not a sign of immaturity. In one of his plays, George Bernard Shaw has a young man ask an eighty-year-old dowager, "How old must a woman be before she ceases to be interested in sex?" Her answer is, "I don't know yet." The recent increased attention to the emotional needs of retired people—as the population grows older—has shown that many a marriage of two elderly people is not only for companionship but definitely includes sex—and whether those elderly people are mature or immature is surely not what makes the difference.

Along with an overinterest in sex often comes an overuse of words of sexual meaning, or of generally "dirty" meaning, as used in swearing. The very use of such words is nowadays supposed to signal sophistication—of some kind! Still, mature people also swear. Both for men and for women, the violence (and the "forbiddenness," so to speak) of swearing can be a useful means of letting off steam and possibly avoiding an explosion into physical violence. The prudish will avoid swearing at all costs, and will generally avoid any mention of sex if they can help it. And, as often as not, the excessively prudish are immature.

The sophisticated, then, may be mature or they may be fixedly immature, or they may be on the way to becoming mature. But in our exploration of what maturity is *not*, let us see quite clearly that it is never to be wrapped up in nothing more than sophistication.

Does maturity "rub off" upon one if one keeps company with mature people? There is probably some transfer of attitudes from one mind to another, but surely it is not necessary to keep the company of the mature in order to make one's self mature. Some very mature people have proved otherwise.

Consider Immanuel Kant, the father of nineteenth-century philosophy—and influenced by Moses Mendelssohn, by the way. From the day of his birth to the day of his death he never traveled more than sixteen miles from his home in the village of Koenigsberg. His association with thinkers must have been very limited. He had no access to large libraries. And yet he has left us two monumental works, *Critique of Pure Reason*, and *Critique of Practical Reason*, that have become cornerstones of modern thought. Limited as Kant may have been in his physical surroundings, his immensely mature mind soared limitlessly in the realms of reason.

Abraham Lincoln was a very lonely person all his life. As a boy, in a log cabin, he had few books from which to study and no learned associates from whom he himself might learn. As a man, he kept on being a "loner," seeming always to draw his attitudes and decisions from within himself. Yet we know him as one of the most mature men in all recorded history.

Maturity, then, may be found within one's self with little or no aid from anyone else—although one should not say that this applies to every type of personality. On the other hand, it is extremely immature to live by and for one's self alone. A popular play of some decades ago, *Craig's Wife*, told the story of a supremely selfish woman. She planned to disassociate herself from everyone, even her husband, so that she would not have to be bothered by people. She succeeded better than she had planned. A key line in the play tells the story: "People who live to themselves are generally left to themselves." This is quite different from the "loner" like Lincoln or like Albert Schweitzer, who is a great humanitarian, genuinely concerned with the human race.

The hail-fellow-well-met type is often lonely underneath and trying to compensate for it. There are thousands of men, women, and children who always remain "loners" in a crowd. Whether an individual lives alone or with others; whether he lives in a small village or in a vast metropolitan center; whether he is an only child or part of a big brood—ultimately his own maturity must come from the depths of his own being. Ripe old age can help him. A great intellect can help him. Education can help him, and in its own way enrich him. Experience can broaden his horizon. Sophistication can sharpen him. Varied association and example can teach him a great deal. Yet he is still in charge of his own maturity. It is up to *him* to make it grow.

Maturity is also not a great many other things. Maturity always comes back to those two great principles; it is a continual state of becoming, and it is shown as one deals wisely with the phenomena of one's life.

Bearing those principles in mind, now let me tell you the story of a man, the father of two children, a boy and a girl. The boy died of cancer at the age of five. The girl, now twelve, had been born completely blind and mentally retarded.

I was in the audience when this man came to the platform to speak. He had recently accepted the presidency of a home for the mentally retarded. The occasion was a fund-raising affair, and its special purpose was to provide an additional wing for the home. The new wing would serve the needs of doubly afflicted children like his daughter.

He told of the tragedies in his family, and I was shocked. Then I found out why he had spoken of them, for he went on to call them blessings. Deeply moved, I heard him tell—without any parade of suffering or sacrifice—that his blessing was to have the privilege of serving retarded children, God's special children. He spoke with such sincerity and simplicity that, when he had finished, there was not the usual shocked silence that greets the relating of a family disaster; instead, there was spontaneous applause. Surely each of us in that audience of more than a thousand framed his reaction in his own words—but I believe we all knew we had witnessed a display of magnificent maturity.

The second story concerns myself. The more I have delved into the subject of maturity, the more I have realized that all of us, every day, are given opportunities to be mature or to be immature —according to the way we react to circumstance. A mature reaction may at first seem strange because it is not usual. Keep it up, however, and it "sinks in." It is really a form of learning by doing.

One of my earliest conscious "learnings" of maturity involved my driving ability, which, I suppose, was as good as the average. I had been driving for about two years. At any rate, there is no point in supposing that rabbis are necessarily bad drivers! I discovered that my fellow motorists seemed to lose their tempers easily when I was around. I was subjected to volleys of abuse, such as: "What's the matter with you?" "Where'd you learn to drive, if you call that driving?" "What's the matter, are you blind (crazy, trying to kill somebody)?" "Why, you blankety-blank fool, I have a mind to get out of this car and beat you up."

At first, that kind of treatment aroused my own temper and I was tempted to answer in kind. I at least tried to make it clear that it was the other fellow who had better go back to driving school, not I; that if either of us was crazy, it definitely was not I; and so forth. On a few occasions I came close to indulging in physical combat.

One day I realized I was being immature; both childish and immature. I said to myself: Just because someone says I am incapable of safe driving, or that I ought to be put away, doesn't make it so. I should not respond to unreasonable anger with more unreasonable anger. One of these days I really will get into a brawl and my erring fellow motorist and my erring self, both missing a few teeth, will both be locked up.

So I concluded that if I ever again were the target of abuse, I would react in a mature manner. In addition, I resolved I'd develop so much skill and care in driving that I'd be a positive model for others. Since that day of deliberate decision, I have rarely been subjected to even an angry look. I drive with far more

confidence. And I feel far more confidence in my ability to see myself and help myself in every way to *become*.

There is nothing new in this. As an example of learning maturity, Epictetus (born around A.D. 60) offers a very practical suggestion: "If you would not have an angry temper, then do not
feed the habit. Give it nothing to help it increase. Be quiet at first
and reckon the day in which you have not been angry. I used to
be angry every day; now every other day; then every third or fourth
day; and if you miss it so long as thirty days, make a sacrifice to
God."

By now you have been reminded several times of the two major
premises that form the framework of maturity. Now we proceed
with a more detailed examination of this subject of many facets,
each one important in our lives. I have been much interested in
searching out every kind of definition of maturity, and especially
listings of the qualities of maturity given us by some very capable
observers. In the next chapter I shall present ten major pillars of
maturity. Know these pillars, see how they support the entire grand
edifice, and you will be better able to make maturity an ever-avail-
able constructive force in your life.

Chapter Three

TEN PILLARS
OF MATURITY

Recently I read a review of Eugene O'Neill's posthumously produced play, *More Stately Mansions*. Struck by the significance of the play, the reviewer mused upon the dismal effect we receive from a building left unfinished.

> When I was about 17 [he wrote], a large apartment building began to go up across the street from where I lived, and within a month or two the Depression struck. Halfway up to its promised six or seven stories, with brickwork rising at irregular heights and with windows marked out like the teeth in a jack-o'-lantern, the building stopped. No men came back to work; no money was ever found to put flooring into the vast cavity. And every day I passed newness that was turning into oldness without having once been used. In due time, three or four years later, the world began to move again and with this movement came the wreckers. Nothing could be salvaged; not the wings that met at rectangles, not the stone that framed a courtyard, not the blind intricate foundations that scurried maze-like, unidentified and uncrowned, inside the shell. I always felt wistful about that building.

As with buildings, so it can be with human beings. I feel sad when I see them standing around uncompleted. Unlike buildings, they could have helped themselves—could have done so much for themselves! At the very least, they could have taken better care of their bodies, and thus have enjoyed better health and lived longer. Or, with more education and more exertion of their latent mind-power, they might now hold better jobs, have more income, and achieve that feeling of security that helps us enjoy life. And above all, such uncompleted persons might have developed all or nearly all of their full maturity potential. Then they would have become not only built to their full stature but also beautifully furbished within and without. Yet there they stand, full of jagged, un-completed edges, only one or two stories high instead of the allotted seven.

Man, ever *becoming*, finds a natural goal in change and growth. Not only the core of maturity is inborn. We are also given a capacity—an innate skill—to develop ourselves toward ever-larger stages of achievement.

It is important to remember that every human being has the core and the capacity, and that the built-in skill waits, ever ready, no matter what his self-neglect or his outwardly inflicted handi-caps may be.

The story of the retarded child is a case in point. For centuries we put him away out of sight; we assumed that his condition was hopeless and helpless. But now we realize that even his affliction cannot completely lock the door to his seed of maturity. That door still can be opened a few inches, in some cases a few feet—which lets a good deal of sunlight come in to stir the seed into waken-ing. We need only bring him the proper forms of therapy, hand him fitting tools and techniques, and he comes at least some distance out of his darkness and almost literally can be seen to blossom.

In my own work with such children, these miracles of dawning have given me my greatest reward. And, because the seed waits so patiently, the plant of maturity can still grow in an adult. The manager of a paper factory told me about the great success he has had in training mentally retarded men and women to perform simple tasks. Bear in mind that previously people of this mental level had been left to waste on the scrap-heap of humanity. Now, in some way, they had become successful. Every week they brought home money they had earned. They felt the inward lift of self-respect. They were happy; and don't ever think that *your* way to be happy is the only way to be happy. Again it is a matter of becoming—not Moses, nor, in modern parlance, the high man on the totem pole—but the best possible Zusya or whatever your name may be.

I promised you Ten Pillars of Maturity. I paused to make sure you know that *you* have the the foundation for those pillars. And *you* can find the walls and floors and ceilings, the sunlit windows and pleasant terraces with which you can nobly complete your mansion.

Now turning from foundation concepts, let us see how some learned and concerned people set up the beams and building blocks of maturity. You will note many interesting parallels, some differences in emphasis, and an overall sense of talking about the same thing. As you read the following lists, I suggest you read with a pencil in your hand. Check off the qualities you believe you see in yourself. Or, if you want to use question marks here and there, make them big and think about them.

Shortly before his death a few years ago, the renowned Dr. Will Menninger suggested his own Seven Criteria of Emotional Maturity. They are:

1. Having the ability to deal constructively with reality
2. Having the capacity to adapt to change
3. Having a relative freedom from symptoms that will produce tensions and anxieties
4. Having the capacity to find more satisfaction in giving than receiving
5. Having the capacity to relate to other people in a consistent manner, with mutual satisfaction and happiness
6. Having the capacity to sublimate; to direct one's destructive and hostile energy into creative and constructive outlets
7. Having the capacity to love

In his book *Emotional Maturity*, another distinguished psychiatrist, Dr. Leon J. Saul, suggests his own eight criteria:

1. Achieving individual independence, especially from parents
2. Factual understanding of the function of sex
3. Accepting the necessity to face reality
4. Having the ability to adapt to change
5. Giving more than receiving
6. Getting rid of hostilities
7. Pouring one's self into constructive activity
8. And above all, loving others

Now let us confer, as it were, with another kind of student of human nature, Dr. Robert N. McMurrry. It is Dr. McMurry's business to analyze and evaluate the competence of employees in large companies—all the way from the stock room to the executive suite. In his *How to Recruit, Select and Place Salesmen,* he suggests eleven criteria of emotional *im*maturity. Let us now look at maturity from the "anti" side:

1. To see money or material things as ends in themselves— not merely as means
2. To accord undue importance to pleasure (Caution: here one must distinguish between pleasure and happiness.)
3. To live only for the immediate present
4. To commit yourself to the world of fantasy (or: become a pathological liar)
5. To behave as if one were all-powerful
6. To be undisciplined in action
7. To be unwilling to accept responsibility
8. To be generally too independent
9. To dodge the acceptance of blame
10. To refuse to learn from the lessons of logic and appearance
11. To be resistant to seeing one's self as one really is

I have carefully surveyed the best criteria of maturity and immaturity I have been able to find, gathered from a variety of sources. Out of these, my own studies, and my own experience in dealing with people, I have quarried my own Ten Basic Pillars. They are:

1. A sense of reality
2. The quality of flexibility
3. A reasonable feeling of independence
4. Willingness to accept responsibility
5. Enthusiastic confidence in one's self
6. Self-discipline (or self-control)
7. Decisiveness of purpose
8. An abundance of love
9. Patience and the courage to be patient
10. The light of hope

These are the strong pillars that are "musts" for your mansion of maturity. With them, all else in the mansion fits firmly into place. Without them the structure is bound to be precarious and incomplete.

Let us examine more closely the inner structure of each sturdy pillar:

1. REALITY

The difference between a neurotic and a psychotic has been defined as follows: A neurotic and a psychotic both see castles in the air; the neurotic worries about them, the psychotic goes right ahead and moves in.

Less jocularly speaking, Dr. Leon Saul warns: "A distorted sense of reality impairs the effectiveness and enjoyment of work and life. It creates a sense of insecurity and inferiority and leads to frustration, fear and hate."

Mature people are often capable of flights of fancy, but they take up their permanent residence in the world of fact. They may exercise their imaginations from time to time, but they deal with this world as they know it—the solid, sometimes hard-to-take land of what is and what must be. The immature are not necessarily mentally disturbed and may not be noticeably neurotic; but they still look at life from an essentially childish level; and that is not the kind of world in which to grow up constructively.

The reality of the unborn infant is one of utter sustained comfort. Once he is born he cannot know that kind of reality again. He is not very old before he learns that he cannot always have what he wants; that not everyone will give him an automatic response of love. He finds out too the sorrow of bereavement; on one level the loss of a special garment or a treasured toy; on another the loss of a pal dog; on yet another level the utter disappearance in death of a father or mother or grandparent or sibling or friend.

Quite often I am asked whether a child as young as six or eight should attend the funeral service of someone who was dear to him. My answer is "Yes." I stress the child's need to face up to reality from the beginning. I believe that children need to participate in human experiences rather than be carried along in a succession of mysteries that may prevent them from seeing their world with wide-open eyes.

Ashley Montagu has suggested that we should do away with the anti-anxiety pills that physicians often prescribe. He suggests that in some cases we may need anxiety pills, to teach someone who needs the lesson that absolute peace of mind is a myth. In this connection, I wonder if too many parents do not surround their children with too much of an atmosphere of anti-anxiety—too much of that essentially good commodity, Tender Loving Care. An overdose of "TLC" can result in the child's growing up (physically but not mentally and emotionally) as the victim of a womb fantasy, feeling that his mother or even both parents will shelter him forever and that they stand ready to ease his hurts and solve his problems for all his days.

This is the explanation of much of bachelorhood and "living with mother." This is where the recent bride, finding that marriage makes demands upon one's maturity, goes home to the womb—that is, to Mother. This often is preceded by a honeymoon fantasy, My experience has taught me that a large proportion of brides and grooms do not have a happy honeymoon. Any honeymoon is a withdrawal from the world. As a temporary state, it will not hurt mature people, and of course a honeymoon can be, and often is, delightful. Yet it can also be followed by a bumpy descent from never-never land!

Fantasy also marches heavily into the world of "success" and gets in the way of many a man's becoming really successful. Some generations ago, Horatio Alger books, then Frank Merriwell books and the like, gave boys a distorted view of achievement. In our own time, the Green Hornet, the Lone Ranger, Batman, and their ilk keep on encouraging the same fantasy. Heroes are few; hard workers are many. The mature person watches out, not for the pie-in-the-sky adventure that may make his fortune, but for ways in which he can logically and consistently "make his own breaks."

2. FLEXIBILITY

That wise Greek of ancient times, Heraclitus, saluted the inevitability of change by telling us you cannot bathe in the same stream twice. The law of change has been seen as a core law of the universe. Thus the human being—like a high-rise structure—must be able to sway with stress, for if he stands rigidly, he may be overturned.

Marriage serves as a fine example of maturity at work. In marriage particularly it is important to sway a little and give a little. (And realize that in a happy marriage, neither party is *always* happy.) Bride and groom come from different backgrounds; how can they think precisely the same way? Parents and children are products of different generations; how can they view the world through the same eyes?

Often I hear inflexible people say that there is only one way to do things right. Do not accept this as an all-embracing truth. Note, rather, that a well-trained and experienced person in any field knows many ways to do his job right, according to the demands of circumstance.

With football having become the highly organized sport it is, formations are mapped out, the opponent is scouted, individual players are studied in even psychological depth, ready-made answers are provided for every attack; in short, the sport comes close to being a science.

That is, until the teams are on the playing field. Then the

quarterbacks must constantly adapt and change their tactics. And the broken-field runner adjusts himself every instant to a changing situation as he dashes down the field.

Again, the skilled surgeon has studied the X rays before he makes an incision; he knows what every organ looks like and where it is placed within the body. Yet still he adapts and adjusts to changing conditions in the patient's pulse and other vital functions. Or he may find something the X ray could not show. Every operation, no matter how well planned, challenges both the surgeon's trained skill and his flexibility.

It is said that the best way to achieve a goal is to have a firm idea of the goal always in mind; to know beyond doubt where you are going. Let this be done rigidly, however, and the goal can be lost. There is great value in the mature ability of changing your course when you must: of shifting to a lower gear when surmounting a steep hill of life; even of turning back and looking for another road when your chosen road turns out to be impassable. A fundamental aspect of maturity lies in putting all the circumstances of your life in proper perspective.

3. INDEPENDENCE

Someone has pointed out that "humans are children for so long that they never get over it." Much of the struggle of adolescence results from the conflict between the developmental drives to be independent and the regressive attraction to the protection and dependence so long enjoyed in our undeniably long childhood.

Surely it is gratifying to the child to find himself one day walking alone, unaided by props or parents. Soon he is roaming into every corner, opening the drawers and cupboards, and even slipping outside the house when nobody is looking. We rejoice with him in his new-found powers. If this is the beginning of a gradual —and occasionally accented and dramatic—breakaway into independence, it is good.

Now consider the average young man or woman while in high school, or better yet in college, when he is really adult in years.

For the most part, such young people are still dependent upon their parents for their food, clothing, and shelter, even if they are living away from home. Yet still they need to be independent. No wonder we have family wars about the establishment of independence in personal action, in politics, in morals, in travel, in attitudes toward war, in religion!

The mature parent will show his child that independence should gradually and not too quickly replace dependence. As mature and civilized people, we have to recognize that absolute independence, like absolute liberty, is a myth. "No man is an island entire unto himself." We depend upon others not only for food, clothing, and shelter, but also for love and friendship and comfort and counsel.

How to be independent as a person and yet maturely dependent in one's relationships with others is an art which only maturity can achieve. I never shall forget the statement of a multimillionaire Kentucky lumberman. When people referred to him as a self-made man, he answered simply: "There is no such thing as a self-made man. Those who work with a man help make him."

4. RESPONSIBILITY

The child puts up a determined resistance against the acceptance of responsibility. He finds it painful to acknowledge blame for misdeeds and mistakes. The water is left running in the bathtub; a window is broken; a spitball is thrown when the teacher has turned to the chalkboard. Questions bring instinctive don't-blame-me answers: "I didn't do it." "I don't know anything about it." Or, when caught red-handed: "I didn't mean it." "My brother made me do it." "The rock slipped out of my hand."

Rare is the child who accepts the responsibility for his actions. That is why the story about George Washington and the cherry tree—whether it be a fact or a Parson Weems fable—has persisted all these years. Father finds cherry tree chopped down and asks his son who did it. The son fearlessly replies, "Father, I did it with my little hatchet." How many thousands of chocolate hatchets are sold each Washington's birthday! And how many Americans know that thus they celebrate the fact that a child *can* be mature?

As we are not all Moses, so are we not all Washington. This is just as well! Really, there is nothing wrong with the ordinary behavorial phenomena connected with childhood. It is only when such behavior extends beyond childhood that there is cause for concern. And the unwillingness to accept responsibility—the desire to evade any possible blame—is also a blatant sign of *adult* immaturity.

So we have the teenager who blames his companions for getting him into trouble with the law. Later, the same person may be a college student who blames his scholastic failure, not upon his failure to study, but upon his bad luck in having to be taught by inferior professors. And later he may be the husband who blames his lack of business success on his wife's failure to encourage him. Or she may be the wife who blames her sloppiness and failure to manage on her husband's lack of an income in the six-figure bracket.

Now, "responsibility" means more than accepting blame when blame is due. It also refers to one's willingness to accept difficult or unpopular jobs or assignments. Above all it means a willingness —when one is fitted—to accept the responsibility of command where the acceptance of blame and obloquy goes right along with the acceptance of glory. There are many executives, however, who will look for a chance to blame some subordinate when the executive himself pulls a "boner" that costs his company a great deal of money. In politics and international affairs, whatever may happen is too often the other fellow's fault.

How well I remember a few significant words spoken by that mature man, John F. Kennedy, after the disastrous Bay of Pigs battle. He said to the world, "I alone am responsible for this tragic error."

Many qualified people will not accept a high post in business, politics, education or elsewhere because they are afraid they will fail—and failure performed in a bright light is no pleasant experience. The truly mature person knows, however, that complete, unvarying success is not only close to being impossible, but also it is no criterion of whether a man has succeeded in an overall way. Reliability, industry, integrity, bravery, and the honest knowledge that one is prepared to do the task required—these form the granite matrix from which we hew this pillar.

5. CONFIDENCE

"Self-confidence," said Samuel Johnson, "is the first requisite to complete undertaking." Emerson wrote: "Self trust is the first secret of success," and "Self trust is the essence of heroism."

One of La Rochefoucauld's supreme maxims is: "The confidence that we have in ourselves engenders the greatest part of what we have in others." In his essay on self-reliance, the ever-quotable Emerson says: "There is a time in every man's education when he arrives at the conviction that envy is ignorance; that imitation is suicide; that he must take himself for better or for worse as his portion; that though the wide Universe is full of good, no kernel of nourishing corn can come to him but through the toil bestowed on that plot of ground that is given to him to till. The power that resides in him is new in nature and none but him knows what this is which he can do. Nor does he know until he has tried."

The quality of confidence has engaged great minds since the dawn of civilization. It always has been recognized as a touchstone of ability; a quality that makes every skill and every effort worth more. Yet here again, in viewing another of the Ten Pillars of Maturity, we cannot deal in an absolute. There is no such thing as absolute certain confidence in one's self nor in any other person. We may have perfect confidence in the daily rising and setting of the sun, in the progression of the changing seasons; or in the pull of gravity—but not in human affairs. Confidence is essential but it must be qualified by common-sense caution. Mature confidence is always qualified by mature caution—and gets notable results.

When you hear children or adults say such phrases as, "Anything I say or do is wrong, so I'll stop trying," "I guess I just don't have what it takes," or "I never get a break. Everything goes against me," you are listening to the voices of immaturity. Confidence is that quality in maturity that does not accept the concept of an overall character inadequacy, does not parade inferiority almost as a virtue, and does not expect defeat.

Confidence, however, is not conceit. A conceited person is not realistic. One can be quietly confident in one's proved talents or in the record of one's achievement; one can say so, and be quite mature in the saying. Recently I heard Truman Capote state in a television interview that when he was a boy, his schoolmates respected him for his dignity and intelligence. The impression was one of honesty and self-confidence; not conceit.

In his biography *Dag Hammarskjöld: A Spiritual Portrait,* Sven Stolpe quotes part of an academy speech Dag made about his own father. Stolpe says these words are actually applicable to the son:

"A mature man is his own judge. When all is said and done his one firm support is his loyalty to his own convictions. The counsel of others may be welcome and valuable, but it does not release him from responsibility; therefore, he must risk being accused of stiff-necked self-sufficiency."

And already, as a youth, in the late 1920s, Hammarskjöld had written: "What you have to attempt is to be yourself." Of a friend whom he greatly admired, he said, "He bore failure without self-pity and success without self-admiration. Provided he knew that he had paid his uttermost farthing, it would not matter to him how others judged the result."

Such externals as failure or success did not disturb Hammarskjöld so long as he knew his inner spirit was pure. It is only the immature who are constantly plagued by guilt feelings or a sense of inferiority or unworthiness. Immaturity then often leads to exaggerated braggadoccio, aggressiveness, and unwarranted competitiveness. If you study a very aggressive child who brags and boasts a lot, you frequently find that he is covering up a feeling of inadequacy as he competes with his parents, schoolmates, or playmates.

The mature person is conscious of his strength as well as his weaknesses. And he backs up his own strengths. What he knows, he knows well. Where he is particularly capable, he knows it, and does not envy another person who, in the same field, may be even more capable.

The mature person sees too that a weakness in one direction need not take away from a strength in another direction. The horse cannot fly like a bird; but, then, a bird cannot pull a wagon. The fish was not fashioned to live on land like a man, but it can far outswim any man and will not drown under water.

Once again we see the necessity of being the best possible Zusya —or whoever you happen to be.

6. CONTROL

Confidence as a pillar of maturity is self-confidence; control as another pillar is self-control.

The Talmud tells a parable about a wily fox who outwitted himself. He found an unattended vineyard, with luscious grapes visible just beyond a high fence. He could not jump over the fence. At last, however, he discovered a small hole in one of the boards of the fence. He squeezed and squirmed his way through it. Nobody came through the vineyard, and for three days the fox lost himself in uncontrolled gluttony, gorging himself with the luscious ripe grapes.

At last, unable to bear the sight of another grape, he staggered to the hole in the fence and tried to crawl through. Alas! His stomach was so stuffed and paunchy that he could not get back through the small hole. How was he to make himself smaller? There was nothing to do but fast. And fast he did, for seven full days. Only then was he able to get out—as thin as he had been when he had come in. He had suffered so much that it quite wiped away his gluttonous pleasure.

This is a fable; but in fables there is much truth. To this very day, in South Africa, they catch monkeys in the following manner: A narrow opening, just wide enough to admit a monkey's extended paw, is bored into a heavy coconut. This coconut is left on the ground in the forest. When a wild monkey comes upon the coconut he sees a chance to get a fistful of its pulp. Eagerly he inserts his paw into the hole and grabs all the pulp it can hold. But when he tries to withdraw his fist, it is trapped inside the shell. Since he will not let go of the pulp, his paw, filled as it is, remains larger than it was when it entered. He cannot, therefore, get rid of the coconut. When the trapper approaches, the monkey tries to run away. Encumbered by the coconut, he cannot go very fast and is easily captured. Yet in captivity, he still refuses to open his fist. The trapper has to break the nut in order to separate nut and monkey.

Now bringing the matter up to the human state, we see something of nearly the same nature occurring; at least, with children. That keen observer, Epictetus, both describes the situation and gives us a useful moral when he says:

"When children thrust their hands into a narrow jar of nuts and figs, if they fill their hands they cannot get them out again. Then they begin crying. Tell them to drop a few nuts and they will be able to get out the rest. And tell them also to drop their desire. Do not demand too much and you will attain."

Self-control applies as well to the control of one's temper; one's passions. You can note in many a person that the inability to control desire—whether for a super-large handful of goodies or for some more "grown-up" treat—is often coupled with the inability to control emotion.

When a child faces a firm "No" he may sulk, throw a tantrum, or threaten to run away. There is a story of a ten-year-old who, having been severely scolded by his parents and denied something he wanted, said, "If you treat me that way, I'll tell my psychiatrist on you."

Yet the same immaturity, different only in its documentation, will show itself in adults as well. Men and women who are thwarted, even in some unreasonable demand, may go into uncontrollable rage, along with tears, wild threats, or even blows. Or they may resort to some sort of reprisal. Reason flies out the window— perhaps all the more so when the temper-loser knows, deep down, that he cannot support his unreasonable demands with logic. But still he cannot let them go!

As with the fox, the uncontrolled person ends up in some way defeated. And as with the fox, the defeat generally comes from placing too high a value on *things*. Epictetus wrote: "He that is to be subdued by man must first be subdued by things. He, therefore, of whom neither pleasure nor pain nor fame nor riches get the better . . . whose slave can he ever be?"

How can one attain such power of mature self-control? First: avoid attaching yourself to anything or anyone as though that thing or person were your permanent possession. Love can be deep, lasting, and true—yet it can avoid the possessive uncontrolled imprisonment that it sometimes becomes.

Second: Accept joys or sorrows as pleasures or pains in their place—which is a passing place.

Third: Do not overdramatize your needs or your desires, your reactions or your passions. Nothing reaches the area of true tragedy except your failure to be yourself.

7. PURPOSE

A dear friend, hale and hearty in his eighty-eighth year, tells me that at about the age of twelve he felt strongly that he had found the goals of his entire life. This is unusual, but now and then a young person is unmistakably dedicated by some inner urge toward music or art or dancing or some other pursuit; or toward a particular goal no matter how far away.

My friend went through many trials and tribulations, but he stuck to his goal and he found it. He was a mature person; he always flexibly found a new path whenever any old path was closed to him. He possesses great wealth and shares it generously. He now spends much of his golden age teaching teenagers the value of having purpose and direction.

Even retarded men and women achieve much more quickly and happily when they can work on a clear-cut schedule toward an objective that is possible and meaningful in their eyes.

Most of us become more mature, more courageous, and more effective when we are caught up in some cause that focuses our wills. The people of England, young and old, found a great reservoir of common maturity of purpose during the blitz of World War II. Hammered by bombs and ravaged by fire, they rallied to repel the threat of Nazi destruction. The people of Israel have rallied more than once, first to create their nation, then to save it, and they have won against formidable odds.

In his novel *The Chosen*, Chaim Potok has a wise old man say:

> I learned a long time ago that the blink of an eye is nothing. But the eye that blinks—that is something. A span of life is nothing. But the man that lives that span, he is something. He can fill that span with meaning, so its quality is immeasurable though its quantity may be insignificant. . . . A man must fill his life with meaning; meaning is not automatically open to life. It is hard to fill one's life with meaning; merely to live, merely to exist, what sense is there to it? A fly also lives.

In maturity there is meaning; in maturity there is purpose. Maturity demands purpose—high purpose.

8. LOVE

Shall we call love, self-love? Not really, for the essence of love lies in its being given and received, shared together. Yet in love there is a strong element of self-love that is not selfish nor egoistic, but necessary to the full mature development of one's being.

Here are two instances:

A successful teacher of a class of "weight watchers" keeps on telling her class: "Love yourself more than you love food." Here, in wholesome self-love, comes the strength of self-control that is so necessary if the overweight person is to get rid of his unattractive, unhealthful burden of excess tissue.

The other instance is taken from *Peace of Mind*, that very successful book by Joshua Loth Liebman. In a chapter called "Love Thyself Properly," Rabbi Liebman tells of a prominent social worker who received an urgent letter from a wealthy society woman, offering her services in a drive toward bettering the conditions under which poor children live. Much of the society matron's letter dealt with her lack of qualification and her imperfections; she spent a good deal of energy in downgrading herself. She concluded, however, that her love of children might make up for her own deficiencies.

The reply she received was pointed and terse: "Dear Madam: Your truly magnificent shortcomings at present are too great. Nothing could prevent you from visiting them on victims of your humility. I advise that you love yourself more before you squander any love on others." Perhaps this reply was too brusque, but it shows a professional recognition of the fact that out of healthful self-love we find the true human warmth that enables us truly to love and benefit others.

Many children have been loved to death—the death of the best part of their own personalities. I was told recently about two brothers. The older had been treated realistically by his parents, and learned to work and to take on responsibility. When the younger brother came along, after quite an interval, there had come a change in the family's fortunes and this child was continually swaddled in affection and protection. At an age at which the older brother had been working, the younger brother spent his time fishing and hunting. And yet, later, the younger brother insisted that his parents had not loved him. He had personality troubles that never afflicted the older brother, and said, rightly, that his parents had so smothered him with love that now he could not give love to anyone, but only was capable of absorbing it.

One of the world's best experiences is to share love with a spouse, and in this sharing to give one's love freely, fully, and confidently. Yet the generous giving of love can only come from a person who confidently loves himself—for then is he wealthy in love, has much to give, and still finds his treasure chest of love always overflowing.

9. PATIENCE

Impatience is a clear and concrete mark of immaturity. We understand and sympathize when the child is impatient to become an adolescent; but when the adolescent simply cannot wait to

become a man, he is showing signs of immaturity. It does not stop
there. The immature man becomes (always is!) impatient to
launch himself upon a career; nor can he wait, and take time to
enjoy life, until he has become quickly successful. All along he is
impatient if anything in his life is the least bit less than beautiful,
and so he constantly makes himself unhappy. And now, in his
forties, he is impatient with his age. Oh, to be young again! By the
time he is seventy, he is impatient with the progress of each day—
both because it takes too long and because it brings him closer to
his end. Yet meanwhile the maturely patient man has lived the
same number of years ripely, fully, and successfully in a way that
the impatient person never can know.

Divorce has many causes, yet behind much divorce lies the one
great immaturity of impatience. Mature people have the patience
and understanding to allow them to wait long enough to become
accustomed to each other's ways; to find adjustments in the matters of sex, money, and temperament. Others give up and get out
—and tend to go through the same futile routine again and again.

Patience, in fact, has saved many a life—while impatience has
ended it before its time. I have conducted funerals for a number of
men and women, young and old, who were suicides—but whom
patience might have saved. Some were stricken by a disease that
appeared incurable, but for which a remedy was found shortly
after they had taken their own lives. Some faced the prospect of
scandal and shame because of some crime or misdeed; yet they
might have been delivered from its consequences if they had
waited. Some sorrowed terribly over the loss of a loved one and
took their own lives, not waiting with patience for the natural
course of emotions to heal the wounds of grief.

In a rabbinical commentary on the Book of Leviticus we can
read how the two sons of Aaron, the high priest, were marching
in a religious procession not far behind Aaron and Moses, when
they were overheard to say resentfully: "If only those old men
would die so that we could take over the leadership of the people!"
The two young men were put to death for bringing strange fires to

the altar of the Lord—the strange fires of presumptuous impatience. There is a certain rhythm in life that bears one strongly along with it if one accept it, but can damage or destroy one if he will not accept it. Impatience puts you out of tune with life. The mature, who really enjoy life—they are patient.

10. HOPE

You may remember the Grecian myth about Pandora (Greek for *all-giving*), the first woman. Prometheus had stolen fire from heaven and had bestowed it as a blessing upon man. Angered, Zeus commanded Hephaestas to fashion a woman out of earth to whom the gods would grant their choicest gifts. Hephaestas gave her song and the art of flattery. Zeus gave her a jar, the so-called Pandora's box, containing all kinds of human qualities, evil and good. Zeus sent Pandora as a gift to Epimetheus, the brother of Prometheus. Despite warnings to accept no gift from Zeus, Epimetheus married Pandora. Pandora could not resist opening the jar. Out flew all kinds of evils and miseries which have remained to plague man. When the lid was clamped down on the jar, only one human quality remained, and that was hope.

Where would we be without our precious store of hope? There used to be a picture in many homes that showed a beautiful young woman playing a harp. All the strings of the harp had been broken but one. Yet this one she played. The title of the picture was *Hope.*

Paul Tillich, in one of his last sermons, "The Right to Hope," voiced his wonderment that today's philosophers and theologians seldom speak of hope. In an article entitled *What Hope for Hope?*, Leon J. Putnam asserts that one of the most hopeful signs of today is the renewal of thinking about hope. But in his book *The Vital Balance*, the psychiatrist Karl Menninger observes that while there are many books on faith and love, there have been few on hope. With all these differing views, there is still the welcome recognition that hope is very important and very necessary to man.

The mature know well that while there is life, there is hope.

These, then, are the ten basic Pillars of Maturity. Fix them firmly, and build upon them the edifice of your life. To become complete it will also need plaster and paint, furniture, curtains, the pictures of loved ones, and other adornments. These matters we shall discuss in later chapters. Only make certain, first of all, that the pillars of your house of life, be it mansion or humble cottage, are set firm and strong.

Chapter Four

YOU
AND THE INNER YOU—I

All of us are subject to innumerable influences, good, bad, and indifferent. Moreover, we may feel the effects of those influences years and decades and generations after they occurred. If you want to blame "influences" for making you whatever you are today, or whatever you are not, you can make quite a case.

In the very beginning of his classic, *Man Against Himself*, Karl Menninger gives an example that shows how deeply and deviously we can trace the roots of any action.

A bank cashier in a small town, after many years of faithful service, is accepted by everyone as a friendly, trustworthy, and honorable man. And yet, after banking hours one afternoon, he locks himself into his office with a revolver. Next morning he is found, a suicide.

Investigation of his books reveals a large shortage. For a long time his friends refuse to believe that such a marvelous man and wonderful father has made away with thousands of dollars of the bank's funds. Forced to face the actual fact, they conclude that he must have become suddenly irrational and yielded to an over-whelming temptation. And then, since he was basically honorable, he was so tortured by remorse that suicide was his only way out.

This did not explain *why* he had taken the money. Some weeks later, the reason appears. This married man had been involved in an affair with another woman. So now everything falls into place: When a solid citizen and trusted employee falls into the clutches of a demanding mistress, he is driven by his passion to buy her everything she desires. He gets the money where he can. Eventually he faces a reckoning—and cannot face it. So it was this mistress, this she-monster, who really killed the poor man.

Enough of an explanation? So it seems, but there still remains the nagging question of *why* such a man, so steady and reliable, should wander into an extra-marital affair. Gradually it appears that a few of his intimate friends knew he had been quite unhappy with his wife. And now the man's physician reveals that the last twenty years of that marriage had been continent because of the wife's frigidity.

Well then, say the loyal friends, it was his wife who really drove the poor man to suicide! She was so cold that she drove him to the other woman, and so to eventual disaster.

But is it not apparent, asks Menninger, that even this cannot explain the entire course of the tragedy? Why did the man marry such a woman? And here, says Menninger, a person who had known the man as a child might explain: "You ought to have known his mother! She was a cold, hard woman, more interested in money then in her children. It's no wonder that he bore life-long influences that made him incapable of making an intelligent marital choice, or of dealing with his mistake in a more competent way. Ah, if only you had known his mother!"

And the mother's mother?

Undeniably we are influenced by matters not of our own making; but just as undeniably we can take hold of our own lives and impress new patterns upon them—patterns of maturity that grow stronger. That is why I speak of *You and the Inner You*. With today's awareness of psychology, many of us turn an old-fashioned "Don't blame me" into a modern "It's not my fault; it's the fault of my environment." Yet all the time, save in drastic cases, anyone can win a conquest over himself. As a great teacher said, "Who is the strong man, the hero, the conqueror? He who controls his passions, his drives, his urges—that is, his inner self."

We remarked before that some highly successful persons seem to get their results by the use of certain childlike qualities. It is just as often apparent that certain childlike qualities (to be precise, immaturities, which, as we know, should not be blamed upon one's merely being a child) keep many a man from truly achieving. The edifice he builds cannot be sound because it is built out of an unsound *self*.

At the height of his baseball career, Babe Ruth, the orphan boy who became the King of Swat, appeared to be slipping. His greatest admirers and closest friends became deeply concerned.

Among his friends was Jimmy Walker, at that time the dapper and popular mayor of New York City. Jimmy gave a dinner in Babe Ruth's honor. He really was trying to save the Babe from whatever it was in the mind atop that great frame that was driving the man toward disaster. When the time came for speeches, Jimmy arose, turned to the guest of honor and said, in essence:

"Babe, we, your friends who admire and love you, are very much troubled. For the past year or so, you have been drinking so much of the beer that comes from Colonel Ruppert's brewery [Ruppert owned Ruth's team, the Yankees] that soon you'll drink yourself out of your eighty-thousand-a-year salary. Babe, you are also destroying yourself as a human being, and as a great symbol, as well as destroying yourself as a baseball player. You know you are the idol of all the youngsters playing baseball in sandlots across the country, and in the schools and colleges of America. They look to you as an example—an example not only of sports achievement, but also of character. Babe, not only for your own sake, but for the sake of all the boys in America, why don't you give up drinking? Why don't you give up carousing until all hours of the morning? Why don't you show them how a real fine man should behave? Don't let them down, Babe."

Babe Ruth was so moved, he cried like a baby. He took Jimmy's hand and promised he would change. The change could be seen in Babe Ruth's actions. Yet really it was a change within his deepest self.

Before you can conquer yourself, you must know yourself. Take a good hard look at the inner *you*. Like an iceberg, most of it floats invisibly below the surface. Only a small part of you shows above the surface. It presents the picture you wish to portray to others. It is your public image on parade. If you are clever—and Babe Ruth was a fairly simple soul—you'll make sure that people like your public image, while only you may know what you are like underneath.

Who knew this better than Jimmy Walker! Perhaps, in trying to help America's hero, he was trying to compensate for what he knew about himself.

Jimmy Walker, handsome, well-dressed, and clever, presided over open corruption in city government and pursued open infidelities in his own marriage. Such was his personality that people elected him and re-elected him, and refused to believe the more and more obvious truth. But the day of reckoning came. Jimmy Walker was impeached for malfeasance of office. The court compelled him to go to Albany, the state capital, for examination.

During a recess, while Jimmy was having lunch with a close friend, the friend asked: "Jimmy, who was your enemy who wanted to do you in? Was it Governor Roosevelt? Was it Judge Seabury? Was it John Haynes Holmes? Was it Stephen Wise?"

Jimmy Walker said, "My one and only real enemy was Jimmy Walker. I did this to myself. There is no one else to blame."

Why do we fail with others? Because we fail with ourselves. A distinguished divorce lawyer told me that the chief basic cause of divorce—not the trimmings—is that one or the other partner of the marriage has not learned how to live with himself.

Now, beginning our examination of you and the inner you, we shall set up a spiritual three-way mirror. Like the mirror milady uses, it enables you to see yourself from every angle.

This three-way mirror will be made up of certain reflecting measurements developed by three different men in three different ages. These men are Marcus Aurelius, the wise and gentle Emperor of Rome in the second century A.D. who was also a philosopher; Rudyard Kipling, England's Poet Laureate in the latter part of the nineteenth century; and Dr. Robert N. McMurry, whom we have already mentioned as a highly successful personnel consultant of our present day. All three have distilled criteria of maturity that can lead us on the way we should go.

Stand yourself within this full-length, three-way mirror. It does not reflect your clothing or your appearance; it reflects the inner you. See what it reveals on every side and from every angle. Honestly face the flaws you detect: the inward features that are unattractive, the faults that are unacceptable. As does the tailor, mark down your own measurements; note where you need a bit more leeway here or a bit less there; that which brings out your best and that which should be re-tailored—from within. This kind of tailoring can do much more for your real "figure" than can any dress or suit of clothes!

Let reflections from the mind of Marcus Aurelius be the front panel of the three-way mirror. His extraordinary maturity has stood the test of 1800 years. His *Meditations* are filled with maxims harvested out of years of experience that brought much frustration and suffering. Also they are born of many years of observation and insight from his rare vantage point of power and prestige. We have selected twenty of Marcus Aurelius's maxims to form the front panel of the mirror.

Let us take them in two sets of ten each, and in the order of their appearance in the *Meditations*. In the first set we have:

1 "FIX YOUR THOUGHTS AS MUCH AS POSSIBLE ON THE VIRTUES OF OTHERS, RATHER THAN ON THEIR VICES."

One of man's most universal traits appears to be his liking for taking his fellow man's virtues for granted and his vices for gossip. This is clearly evident in the usual parlor conversation and newspaper article. People always seem interested in learning why their neighbors may be, not good, but good-for-nothing. Marriages on the rocks are much more fun to talk about than marriages that sail along in smooth water.

Perhaps when we look for the worst in others—perhaps when we are fascinated by a tale of *mis*deeds—we seek to salve our own guilt. Certainly we take an unholy glee in finding out that others are not holy. We set up for ourselves an eleventh commandment: *Thou shalt not be found out.* Or we may prefer Oscar Wilde's wry witticism: "I can resist everything except temptation!"

If your reflection in the silver of this maxim is poor, you have found a flaw that can be remedied. You need not quite imitate the three monkeys who see no evil, hear no evil, and speak no evil: you can, though—short of neglecting to report a crime or a danger —refrain from talking about someone else of whose evil you are aware. Concerning yourself with the vices of others can become a pastime that is damaging to you. In his *Essay On Man*, Pope warns us:

> Vice is a monster of such frightful mien,
> As to be hated needs but to be seen.
> Yet seen too oft, familiar with her face,
> We first endure, then pity, then embrace.

2. "THE BEST WAY OF AVENGING THYSELF IS NOT TO BECOME LIKE THE WRONGDOER."

One of the quickest ways to break up a marriage is for a wife, on discovering that her husband has been cheating on her, to go out and have an affair of her own. The most immature thing a parent can do to a child who has shouted or struck out at him is to shout back or strike back. If there is any justification at all for an employee's stealing from the cash register, the poorest justification is to point out that the employer is dishonest.

Very often children who feel their parents have been unreasonable and unkind will unconsciously seek to cure their hurt by being unreasonable and unkind toward other children. That is not so bad for *children*—although one hopes to show them better. For anyone at any age, the best way to avenge yourself is *not* to behave like the wrongdoer. The all-embracing maturity of returning good for evil is asking too much of the average man. But you can refuse to seek vengeance of an active sort, and you can continue to be a right-doer in your relationship to the wrongdoer and to society. More than a few times, this jolts the wrongdoer onto a path that is right.

It often has been said that when a child does wrong, he should not be told that he is bad. Rather, he should be made to see that what he has done is bad. This can be applied at several adult levels.

Once a pious deacon of a small-town church was conducting the usual prayer in his dining room, just before the evening meal. The quiet, heartfelt prayer was rudely interrupted by some roaring from the next-door neighbors—who were loud and lewd.

"Oh Lord," cried the Deacon, "destroy those sinners!"

Gently, his wife said, "Not so, my dear husband. Let us pray for the death of the sins, not for the death of the sinners." A solid plank for the floor in your house of maturity!

3. "IF ANY MAN DOES WRONG, THE HARM IS HIS OWN."

Quite often, troubled parents bring to my office a bright child who feels he can just coast through school. He is getting C's when he should be getting A's. He'd rather play games or watch television than study.

I point out to him that he is hurting himself. Sometimes I try to make him see that later on he will not be able to blame anyone but himself for not having received the good education that can do so much toward building a good life. But as a rule my words go in one ear and out the other. It is difficult for a child to understand that his neglect of his studies can leave an empty place in his life—a need that may never be filled.

Sometimes a parent can use some dramatic device to put a lesson over. Children like this story: A boy found out he could lie his way out of bad situations, so he went on lying as a quick and easy way of avoiding explanations for the mischief he caused. His father tried desperately to stop him, but with no success.

When the boy came home from school one day, he found a big white post fastened upright in the lawn in front of his house. "I put it there," his father told him. "Every time you tell a lie I shall drive a nail into the post. You'll see those nails every time you go in or out."

The boy continued to lie. The father kept on driving nails into the post. Within three months the post became so full of nails that hardly a white spot was visible. When the boy saw that his father was getting ready to put up another post, he said: "Father, my friends have been asking me about that post and the nails you drive into it. Of course, I lied to them. Now I'm afraid, when they see two posts, they really are going to find out what a liar I am. If I stop telling lies, will you remove the nails?"

"Gladly," the father said. "Every time you tell the truth in answer to a question, I'll take out a nail."

Eventually all the nails were taken out. Now the boy said to his father, "I've stopped telling lies. You have removed the nails. But the holes where the nails were are still there."

"Yes," said the father. "Soon I shall take down the post. But you see, son, we can cover over those holes with putty, smooth the edges, and paint them white again. But the scars of the nails inside the post will still remain." The boy got the point.

As children can learn from adults, so should adults learn from children—by seeing themselves, on occasion, lost in an immature childhood of neglect, self-indulgence, cruelty or outright crime (merely mischief in a child) as much as though they never had grown beyond the age of ten. We have mentioned it before, but here is another facet of the matter—the realization that "if any man does wrong, the harm is his own." To become mature, then, is only to act in the interests of one's self-preservation—no matter how good the temporary advantage of an immature action may seem to be.

4. "SIN IS MAINLY ERROR AND IGNORANCE."

For centuries our western religions have saturated our consciences with depressive and destructive guilt associations about sin. The doctrine of Original Sin, for example, teaches that man's very birth is clouded with sin and can be cleansed of its dark stain only with supernatural help.

Perhaps the three most urgent instincts of man, besides his instinct to preserve his own life, are his sex instinct, his acquisitive instinct, and his aggressive instinct. It is in the area of these instincts that we are most likely to sin—or, let us say, we are most likely to run afoul of someone's notion of *sin*.

It is interesting to note that the Biblical word for "sin," in the original Hebrew, is derived from a root verb form that means *to miss the mark*. Originally, it would appear, if a man shot an arrow at a mark, and missed, he had "sinned."

We are more responsible about handling the idea of sin in its present connotation, but we may still think of sin in the sense of missing the mark—missing the mark, that is, when a man's natural urges drive him toward some goal that is not worthy. Nothing is wrong with the acquisitive instinct when we aim it at making a living in some worthy manner or at honestly acquiring property or other possessions. Again, the aggressive instinct, used to defend us against attackers, is aimed well. Only a sinful *aim* turns an instinct into a sin.

As for sex, precisely the same criterion applies. But sex has a special and vulnerable place, since sex is what most people mean when they talk of sin.

In his *Reminiscences*, Tolstoy tells of a ninety-year-old Cossack who laughed at the author's shyness with young women. "Is it a sin to look at a pretty girl?" said the old man. "Is it a sin to love her? No, my friend, that's no sin, it's salvation! God created you and he created pretty girls too." While this sort of thing can go too far, the general attitude is a healthier one to take than the attitude that sex is always sinful. "Sin is mainly error and ignorance." Don't go immaturely overboard in pointing your finger at so-called sin; maturely draw a line.

5. "WE OURSELVES ARE WEAK AND NOT PERFECT."

In maturity lies the innate acceptance of human imperfection. Only God, or what Matthew Arnold calls "Power Not Ourselves," can be perfect. At least it is so in the ancient concepts, but even these are being challenged by liberal religion. One can believe in God and still question His all-knowing quality. Also, worshipers who have been praying fervently for years—and getting benefit from their prayers in peace of mind and release from care and sorrow—are now questioning whether God hears, and, if he hears, whether He really cares.

Whether or not God is perfect, man has plenty of evidence that he himself is not perfect. It is, in fact, utterly immature—a clinging to the inexperienced attitudes of childhood—to believe that nothing you say or do can be wrong. Trouble lurks in the marriage where the husband believes he is always right—and so his wife always wrong—or vice versa. The boss is not always right. The clergyman, try as he may, is not always right. It is immature to believe that your religion possesses all there is of truth; that your nation is always righteous; or that your child must always be in the right if he has a fight with another kid.

The mature person knows there is no ever-perfect love, no completely blindfolded justice, no absolutely unalloyed goodness, and no happiness that does not trip up now and then. The mature person knows, too, that he can be strong today and weak tomorrow; or that he can know failure after failure, at last attain success, and then know failure again. All he can ask is that he not know failure *within himself*.

If a man's life were perfect he would never experience any frustration or fear, any anxiety or worry, any tension, or any terror. In that case he would hardly be human, and certainly could not understand or appreciate or work with or love other human beings.

You are weak, says the philosopher, and you are not perfect. Once you have learned to live emotionally with this truth, you are ready to take life as it comes to you—and do a far better job of dealing with it, of finding stores of strength, and of winning happiness and success than the person who deludes himself about his own perfection.

6. "A MAN MUST LEARN A GREAT DEAL TO ENABLE HIM TO PASS A CORRECT JUDGMENT ON ANOTHER MAN'S ACTS."

The next time you find yourself at a dinner party or bridge table engaged in general conversation, watch out for quick and authoritarian judgments of events, assessments of individuals based upon insufficient and garbled data, and carelessly gathered products of the rumor mills. The "facts" upon which deep judgments are made are frequently not facts at all. If they are facts, they are generally not put into proper perspective. They are often taken far out of context, and certainly the one who sits in judgment has no knowledge of the motivations of the judged.

Not only is it difficult to pass a correct judgment upon someone else; it is just as difficult and sometimes more difficult to judge one's own self fairly. No man is entirely nothing or entirely something. No one is so low that he cannot rise, nor anyone so high that he cannot sink. We see a man momentarily; how do we know if he (or ourselves)is on the way up or on the way down, or what his mood may be doing to him?

At least you judge yourself to yourself. If your judgment is to be spoken or written—communicated to another mind—how much more careful it must be! A judgment based on nothing more than an impression, or a rumor, or upon one chance meeting, can be very destructive of another person's reputation. Slander hurts three; he who is slandered, he who hears the slander, and the slanderer himself.

Again, a careless recommendation can do harm. As often as not, someone is recommended for some position for no better reason than his being a fellow member of a lodge, for example. Again there is harm done; to the recommended person if he is not suitable for the job; to the person who gives him the job; and to the recommender, who acted with bad judgment—and knew it.

Be thrice careful before judging your fellows. This is maturity; to speak what you believe *with good reason* to be the truth.

7. "WHEN YOU ARE VERY MUCH VEXED OR GRIEVED,
CONSIDER WELL THAT MAN'S LIFE IS BUT A MOMENT
AND AFTER A TIME WE ARE ALL LAID OUT DEAD."

Vexation disturbs. Grief distresses. You cannot avoid them; they will come when they will come. Yet with some people they are so prolonged they become almost a way of life, and one suspects that such people have developed a perverse love of misery.

Some vexation is normal to any life. So long as men and women are fashioned in the molds of different inheritances and environments, endowed with different capacities and temperaments, and influenced by varying urges and diverse aspirations, so long will they find ways to vex each other. Nor does love guarantee a continual lack of vexation with the loved one. In fact, it is almost bound to happen that husband grates upon wife's peace of mind, brother bothers brother, children and parents get on each other's nerves, or that the best of friends become extremely annoyed with one another.

We mention the situation of the newborn baby at the moment of his first *becoming*. Sometimes it seems that his first tiny cry is an expression of vexation that he has lost his soft watery cradle within the womb. Be that as it may, we certainly can look upon the mite with the sure knowledge that as he grows, so will his problems grow along with his joys, and his vexations and frustrations along with his victories. This tiny six-pound creature will one day know bereavement; he will know the special grief of having a friend let him down; he will experience those times of disaster that seem to touch every marriage; he will have to endure injustice; one day he will be rejected and suffer miserably because of it.

Will he then pause to consider well that man's life is but a moment, and that—to continue in modern parlance—it's only when you're dead that nothing can worry you? Do what you can to give him cheerfulness and courage; let him know that nothing—absolutely nothing—can spoil his life unless he lets it. Then the boy or girl can make of sorrow and annoyance mere incidents that he endures, knowing they are passing, while his life is attuned far more strongly to constructive action and well-earned joy.

There is another fine saying along these lines. "You can't stop the birds from flying over your head, but you can keep them from building nests in your hair." One wonders if this saying is ancient enough for Marcus Aurelius to have known it.

8. "NO WRONGFUL ACT OF ANOTHER CAN BRING SHAME ON US. IT IS NOT A MAN'S ACTS THAT DISTURB US, BUT OUR OPINIONS OF THEM."

This is not to say that a wrongful act of another cannot harm you. Slander leaves a dark stain, hard to erase. Prejudice cuts a deep scar, difficult to heal. Yet, the mature person, dealing wisely with both the pleasant and the unpleasant phenomena of his existence, knows that he is still the same person he always was. You may have been wronged and even physically hurt; but you were not shamed and so, within yourself, you were not diminished.

Marcus Aurelius had a Grecian tutor named Epictetus. As a boy, Epictetus had been sold into slavery and had been cruelly and permanently crippled by his master.

Nevertheless he was not shamed. In his remarkable *Discourses*, Epictetus asserts that it is the mark of a mature man to maintain mastery of himself by not permitting anyone or anything to master him.

> What resources have we [he asks] when the external world beats upon us, whether it be a catastrophe of nature or a quirk of human nature, whether issuing from others or ourselves? The only resource to which we can turn is our own internal will, what else but to distinguish between what is ours and what is not ours, what is right and what is wrong? If I must die, must I die groaning too? Befettered, must I also lament; be exiled, and what hinders me then but that I may go smiling and cheerful and serene? Then I will fetter you. What do you say, man? Fetter me? You will fetter my leg but not Zeus himself can get the better of my free will. I will throw you in prison; I will behead that paltry body of yours. Did I ever tell you I alone had a head not liable to be cut off?

Socrates, the greatest of the Greek philosophers, was condemned to death for what the Establishment said was the crime of teaching atheism and immorality. His conviction brought him no sense of shame, but rather pride. He remained master of his own convictions to the end.

This too was the secret of Gandhi's serenity when he defied the British Empire. Everyone had an opinion of Gandhi's marches of protest, his fastings, his other disturbing acts . . . but of course, "disturbing" is an opinion word. Disturbing or inspiring? Dangerous or much to be desired? Take heed of how much *opinion* goes into your judging of anyone's actions. No mature person can be entirely free of conditioned opinion, a general willingness to be-

lieve that certain things are good and certain things are bad. However, you can look upon your fellow man with sympathy, with an
attempt to understand him, and, above all, with wide-open eyes.

9. "OUR ANGER HURTS US MORE THAN THE ACTS THEMSELVES."

Anger, in its own way, appears to be a divine passion. In the
Bible, God frankly states that He is angry and that He will do
something about it. He sends a flood to wipe out the wicked generation of Noah. He smites Pharaoh with plagues in order to soften
his heart. He tells Amos that for their sins He will destroy nations,
including that of His own people, Israel.

God, however, need not be concerned about his own anger. He
does not have to protect himself from its consequences.

The entire concept of a godlike anger—anger wielded from on
high—serves to point up the fact that man's anger stays with him
at his own level. Man, therefore, has to live with the consequences
of his anger. At times, such as when anger overturns an evil, these
consequences are constructive. Too many of us, however, do not
realize how often anger takes on the nature of a boomerang and
comes back to hurt the man who sent it forth.

Primitive man did not distinguish among the three general aspects of anger: its inner birth, its outward expression, and its self-
destructive nature. When he stubbed his toe on a rock, he would,
like you or me, cry out in pain. But then he would heap curses on
the rock, as if it were some animate evil spirit. He might even
deliberately hit it with another rock in retaliation for the harm it
had done him.

Anger, even when not caused by physical pain, still brings out
physical—and violent—actions in the immature. Children lost in
their own rage will break toys, windows, or whatever else is handy.
Husbands and wives, despite their "grown up" years, will fling
crockery or even furniture. It should be acknowledged that there
is some value at some times in finding a release for anger that
otherwise remains boiling within one, causing unrelieved tensions
that may literally affect one's health, but this mature understand-

ing of the mechanics of anger can point to other more harmless forms of release—perhaps by punching a pillow. Uncontrolled, the physical expression of inward annoyance can cause further physical harm: many a crippled child bears through life the consequences of a parent's wrath over a childlike action. In addition there may be great, often long-term, harm following some bitter, damning verbal expression of anger. The mature person realizes that the effects of his emotions as well as of his actions are two-edged; they impinge upon his own life as well as upon another's.

Displeasure, resentment, or the determination not to be further injured by one who is injuring you can be expressed forcibly and yet without the burden of hatred that adds poison to your message. "He that is slow to anger," says the Bible, "is better than the mighty."

10. "BENEVOLENCE IS INVINCIBLE IF IT BE NOT AN AFFECTED SMILE NOR ACTING A PART."

One of the many stories about Tolstoy—it's hard to say which ones are true—tells that he went out for a walk on one of the coldest of Moscow's white frozen nights. A beggar stopped him and asked for alms. Tolstoy was willing enough to give charity, but now he searched all his pockets and could not find a kopeck. With typical absent-mindedness, he had left all his money at home.

With a sigh of genuine regret, he said, "Brother, I am sorry. I have nothing to give you."

"But you have given me something—something wonderful!" said the beggar.

"Have I?" the puzzled Tolstoy asked.

"You called me brother," said the beggar, with tears of gratitude in his eyes.

Marcus Aurelius died many centuries before Tolstoy was born, yet one feels he would have seen this incident as illustrative of his own words: "Benevolence is invincible if it be not an affected smile nor acting a part." Others have said that in giving, the value of the gift lies not so much in itself as it does in what it carries of the giver. To the half-frozen beggar, who received nothing tangible, came something worth infinitely more—the genuine warmth of the word "brother."

This, then, is the invincibility of benevolence; that it builds a bond between heart and heart. We can see true benevolence in the sincere, unselfish type of person who gives to a cause or to an individual. He is concerned only with the strength of the cause or the welfare of the beneficiary. We can also see the self-aggrandizing type of charity—not really benevolence—that comes from a person who is more concerned with the gratitude he will evoke or the impression he will make.

Yet, though the first type of giving may come from the maturely self-confident person who is capable of real sharing, and the second type from the basically immature person who cannot give unless he receives some ego-polish in return, one must also look realistically at the end results of giving. I have often heard generous givers have their motives questioned. Others grumble that "fat cat" wants to get his name in print and in other ways enjoys basking in the glow that surrounds a benefactor. The days of "Lady Bountiful" are over, the demand for gratitude is passé, and now we know that benevolence is every man's due as well as his duty. With all this, are not the end results as important as the spirit of the giving?

When someone gives, someone else benefits. Especially when the gift is not made from hand to hand, but through some organization or other intermediary, surely the benefit a sum of money can bring is not tainted by the possible smug pride of its giver.

The lesson here is a subtle one, to be most appreciated by mature people. It is this: With the giving of a gift to one who needs it, there is a reflection of the action back upon its source, just as there is with any other action. To the mature mind, this reflection comes as a sense of doing no more than justice. He is not aggrandizing his own opinion of himself; he is doing a duty toward the society that upholds him, and he is satisfied as a member of that society—as a brother to all.

It also requires a high degree of maturity to realize that you are injuring your own soul when you *fail* to help a fellow man. We shall meet this thought again in the next chapter.

Chapter Five

YOU
AND THE INNER YOU—II

The New York Times's humorous but sage observer, Russell Baker, points out that "the psychiatric need these days is to identify. Walk into any room full of strangers, lift a glass, and two swallows later some sadist whose pleasure derives from slashing other persons' eyes will be telling you: 'The trouble with you is that you don't know who you really are.'" Having noted this, Mr. Baker goes on to give it a very valid reverse-twist: "The true formula for happiness is knowing who you aren't. This is something that must be learned gradually, a step at a time. Let us consider, for example, a man who in 1932 was seven years old. At that age it would have been natural for him to have spent long hours under the impression he was Tom Mix. Just as naturally, he would probably have developed the illusion that he was a person capable of actually becoming Tom Mix some day. The only important thing for that man today is that he be under no illusion that he has actually become Tom Mix."

The elder Oliver Wendell Holmes pointed out that when two people are holding a conversation, there are really six people present; there is A as B thinks he is, A as A thinks he himself is, and A as he really is; and there is B similarly divided. So you see, the question of *who* you are is really not an idle question.

And so we return to the one bedrock foundation of *self*—the Inner You. It can be a *self* that is quite different from the outward appearances it prefers to take—or must assume according to circumstance. Marcus Aurelius, adopted by a Roman emperor and an emperor himself, was an aristocrat of enormous power and boundless wealth. Yet he expressed his thanks—not for that wealth—but for the philosophy that helped him develop his maturity and the grace that saved him from sin. There was his true self shining through! He was betrayed by his faithless wife, Faustina, and faced rebellion by his vicious son, Commodus. Yet his maxims show the spirit of sanity and serenity and maturity that stayed with him till the end.

We come now to our second helping at this feast of wisdom, the *Meditations*. The following ten maxims are largely devoted to helping us deal wisely with the phenomena of existence when those phenomena are "ill winds"—events that we call evil.

11. "MAN'S CONCEPT OF EVIL RISES OUT OF HIS INABILITY TO PERCEIVE THE GREAT WHOLE OUT OF WHICH EVILS ARE BUT SUBSERVIENT PARTS."

To know this maxim, and to know it early in life, is to buttress the maturity of one's overall view of life as it comes to one. If you are fired from a job, this evil (as it is to *you* and *at that moment*) in the immature mind may resemble a vast storm area covering a continent. However, to the mature mind, it is more like a little cloud that briefly obscures the light of the ever-radiant sun. The child's broken toy is a tragedy; but he soon gains the experience of life that enables him to see a broken toy for the trifle it is. Yet, as we go along, too many of us seize upon anything that does not please us and call it a disaster; we do not perceive the great whole of life. As someone who could turn a good phrase once said, "We prefer to look at life through mud-colored glasses."

Any judge knows that now and then a character witness will appear before him, utterly bewildered that his friend—who may be sent to jail for some jail-worthy reason—"could have done such a thing."

"Why, your Honor," comes the protest, "I've known George for thirty years and I've never seen him indulge in any kind of violence. . . ." Etc.

And so, if George has now been caught engaged in criminal

violence, his friend insists on taking the long view, the broad-average view of George. George is simply not that kind of fellow. Well, he isn't—on the average—but this time he slipped, and, unfortunately, the judge may look only at this time. Or he *may* decide that George should, after all, be given the benefit of a long-term view of his behavior.

In the same way the long-term view of life is the view by which it is most fairly judged. Often, in clinging to this concept, we perceive that evils have brought some good with them. One should not uncompromisingly accept such sayings as, "Every cloud has a silver lining." Yet, the silver lining is so often not seen because nobody looked for it. And silver lining or not, too much attention was paid to the cloudy days and the rainy days; so much that their attendent worry and care cast shadows into the sunny days as well.

A man's life is the entire stretch of his existence. See it as a journey. Let us say that in the evening you notice a weary traveler, barely able to drag one foot after another, covered with the dust of the road. Who knows what joy he had all day along the way? Who knows what marvelous scenes and delightful experiences he remembers—and what great events he may enjoy tomorrow?

Teach your boy or girl—help them to become mature—by illustrating to them that although life can be beautiful, ugliness is often part of it; that love is glorious but that now and then one will encounter hate; that success is delightful, yet it must be earned, and often there is travail in the earning. "Evils" often are mere unpleasantnesses if one chooses to see them that way. And even actual evils are only subservient parts that serve to set off the goodness of life.

12. "CONSIDER THAT THOU ALSO DOEST MANY THINGS WRONG AND THAT THOU ART A MAN LIKE OTHERS; AND EVEN IF THOU DOST ABSTAIN FROM CERTAIN FAULTS, STILL THOU HAST THE DISPOSITION TO COMMIT THEM."

One might add a codicil to this maxim; a codicil that is inherent in some other of Marcus Aurelius' writings. Thus: the fact is that a rigid adherence to rightness is no guarantee that nothing wrong will happen to you.

Once again it is worth remarking, with a modern spelling of Donne's excellent words, that no man is an island entire unto himself. Now remember the rhyme about the automobile driver who was always right—perhaps a little *too* right . . .

> Here lies the body of Henry Gray,
> Who died defending his right-of-way.
> He was right, dead right, as he drove along,
> But he's just as dead as though he'd been wrong.

So much being said, one might reread the remarks on flexibility in relation to maturity, and consider that many of us consider "right" to be what the law allows us to do. In morals and in matters of plain fairness we often take quite another view. In motoring and other occupations containing some element of danger, we may not be mature enough to see the necessity of doing, not necessarily that which is "right" in the sense of being within our rights, but that which is dictated by common sense.

Let us say, however, that you know "thou . . . doest many things wrong." You need not be in any sense a criminal, but your life simply has not been going right. Well then, you still "art a man like others." There is nothing at all unusual about making mistakes. In fact, there is nothing at all unusual about making the same mistakes over and over. A mature person, however, since he is always *becoming*—changing toward the better—attempts to profit from his mistakes.

Remember there are seven stages of maturity. Let us suppose you are in the fifth stage, that is, you are about forty. By now you have had a good deal of education, both formal and informal; you have had considerable experience; and much exercise in the various sectors of your interests and activities.

In short, you have had sufficient life-experience to enable you to take a good hard look at your life and ask: "*What does it all add up to?*" Then, depending upon your own situation, and sparing yourself no question however painful, you will ask:

"Am I truly happy with my wife or husband? What must I do to improve my marriage? Is there something so basically wrong that we should consider divorce?

"What about my children? As they enter the stage of life in which they think of marriage and careers, is there anything I can do to help them avoid the mistakes that others make—or the mistakes that I have made?

"Am I still friendly with my children—if indeed I ever have been? And if not, how can I become more friendly?

"Am I happy in the means by which I earn my livelihood? What made me go into my business or profession; my honest desire, or some outside influence that I should have resisted?

"I am a businessman; do I really want to be in business? Shall I now pursue the profession of which I dreamed in my youth, even though it means going back to college to get a degree?

"I am in a profession; do I really want to be a professional person? Have I always been uneasy, and so, perhaps, inefficient, in this profession that I entered because my parents pushed me into it?

"I don't like my social group. What keeps me going around with the same old crowd? Shall I establish new friendships? Is it time to pull up stakes, move to a different town?"

We spoke before of a time when a man of forty was old and just about finished. This is so no longer. Whatever may be the defects of our times, we live much longer than we used to and, at forty, almost anyone is still young enough to make a fresh start. Also, at forty, you should be mature enough to make a decision.

If you feel you need expert advice, get it. There are personnel counselors and there are psychiatric clinics. If you live in a small community where you are not sure of privacy, you can find a counselor elsewhere. A clergyman of your own religion, or almost any clergyman, anywhere, can either help you or can put you in touch with the person you need. Or simply check the telephone directory for a clinic, which will often be connected with your local Health Department.

A professional evaluation is worth whatever it may cost. Be mature enough to act. And be mature enough to see that your knowledge of not having lived as constructively as you could have lived is common knowledge to millions of people. To do something

about it—to realize you can "take arms against a sea of troubles"—
is in itself a great becoming.

The second part of the same maxim is, "if thou dost abstain
from certain faults, still thou hast the disposition to commit them."
Yes, we all have the disposition to commit acts that give us some advantage that simply is not our due. To go around feeling guilty
because you have such feelings is to do harm to yourself. The sub-
conscious contains all kinds of violent strivings that, fortunately,
are censored out by the more civilized portions of the mind; and
if these violences and unfairnesses peep through now and then, it
is only to be expected. They show you are not a saint. This should
occasion no surprise!

13. "IT IS NOT FIT THAT I SHOULD GIVE MYSELF PAIN. FOR I HAVE NEVER UNDULY GIVEN PAIN EVEN TO ANOTHER."

It is significant that in the Biblical scheme of the universe it was
not basically planned that man should know pain. God set up man
in the Garden of Eden—a place of perfect happiness. Only after
man ate of the forbidden fruit—the knowledge of good and of evil
—did he know troubles and pain. It is thus in the human conscience that man must *expect* pain. So, as the unique human mind
totaled up more and more centuries of examining the human
state, it often found reasons to sanctify pain and hail it as a virtue.

Examine the origins and rituals of many religions and you will
find that suffering and sorrow play a vital role. A conspicuous
example is the crucifixion of Jesus as explained in the theology of
Christianity, wherein God's only begotten son had to die a cruel
death so that His believers might live.

Physical pain and the emotional pain of self-imposed solitude
have been used for ages as an approach to saintliness. The pleasures
of the flesh and the delights of worldly pursuits are denied in the
name of God. Saints have worn hairshirts and tortured themselves
with self-flagellation and even with mutilation in the service of
their Master.

Enlightened religions now teach that self-inflicted or accepted pain is of no worth to God or man. If God is good, He can find no pleasure in His children's pain. It would seem more in harmony with the universal scheme to believe that man's most blessed pursuit is the exile of pain, even the pain of death, and an attempt to fit himself once more for a life that in some way resembles life in the Garden of Eden.

Unfortunately, religion—as it has been for centuries—tends to keep man imprisoned in a deep sense of inner guilt. Wherever man turns to taste the fruits of pleasure, he too often finds himself confronted by a "Thou shalt not." When so much pain—inescapable, inner soul-pain—is involved in satisfying a hunger for pleasure, it becomes almost logical to eliminate one's pleasures in order to spare one's self pain.

14. "DEATH HANGS OVER THEE WHILE THOU LIVEST. WHILE IT IS IN THY POWER, BE GOOD."

In sensing the true deep meaning of this statement, one needs to be careful of one's approach.

There is first of all the approach exemplified by such men as H. G. Wells. When he was honored by a group of English authors, Wells said he knew he was fortunate to have lived long and knew he soon must die. He said he remembered when, as a child, his nurse would say to him: Master Henry, it's your bedtime." He would protest, of course, even though he knew that sleep would bring him much welcome rest.

"Death," continued Wells, "is a nurse, both affectionate and stern. When the time comes, we protest a little, but we know quite well that the time for rest has come and in our hearts we are longing for it.

John Gunther, after his son lost a long battle with a brain tumor, wrote: "Look Death in the face; it is a friendly face; a kindly face and reluctant, knowing it is not welcome but having to play its part. . . . No fear of Death, no fight against Death, no enmity toward Death. Friendship with Death as with Life."

This is one approach, and I do not like it. I believe it a harmful immaturity to call Death a kind nurse or a good friend or a great blessing—except, perhaps, when Death brings release from ungovernable and incurable pain.

If death, however, is the price we have to pay for the privilege of birth, I have a quarrel with God. If God be all-powerful, might he not have fashioned this earth into a much larger ball so that we never would run into problems of overpopulation? Or could he not insure that fewer children be born—and this as a perfectly natural phenomenon? Why should there be death for man, when all his makeup and resources seem to hold out the promise of living almost eternally? Moreover, it seems evident that with small changes Man could stay vigorous and creative almost forever.

I am not convinced that the optimistic philosopher Leibnitz was correct when he said that ours is the best of all possible worlds. I rather agree with the pessimist who commented that he was afraid it was.

None of this changes the fact that death is here to stay. Maturely, then, using the pillar of *reality* and the pillar of *flexibility*, we can adjust to it.

We can go on to do even better. With some other pillars of maturity, such as responsibility and confidence and purpose, we can concentrate on those factors of *life* that we *can* change.

15. "MANY WHO NOW ARE PRAISING THEE SOON WILL BLAME THEE."

There are times when I am graciously and sincerely thanked for some service I have been able to render. More than that; I am praised. I often say, "Thanks. But remember! Today I'm a hero and tomorrow I may be a bum."

One of the hard realities—and a maturity—of life is the realization that fame is nothing solid; fame yields to blame with no trouble at all. As a conspicuous example of that tragic truth, consider the case of Charles Lindbergh. As a young man, he electrified the world with his solo flight from New York to Paris. He was everybody's hero. But during the 1930s, perhaps embittered by the kidnap murder of his young son, he expressed views that seemed to echo some of Hitler's. He was angrily condemned; condemned as he never would have been if he had not been so famous. Ever since, he has been a man in seclusion.

The mature man will know that praise, like a cigarette, can be enjoyed but may be dangerous. Praise and fame can give you a false sense of security that will not hold up under the pressure of the first mistake you make. And, being human, you will make mistakes! Or, even if what you do cannot be labeled absolutely as a mistake, you will do something that simply puts you in a bad light with too many people.

Remember Woodrow Wilson? Hailed at the end of World War I as the Savior of Mankind, the Apostle of Peace, the modern Messiah? Remember his dream—to have the United States in the League of Nations? And remember how this dream was rejected, and how it hastened his death?

We all learn in school how admired George Washington was for the nobility of his character (whether or not that cherry-tree story is true) and how respected he was as a general and a leader of men. Not many of us know, however, that once he became the first President of the young United States, he was subject to the most terrible vilification and abuse—for the reason, generally speaking, that the President of the United States cannot help but displease large numbers of people. Washington's writings on the subject are almost pathetic; the famous, honest, and well-meaning man protesting in horror at the slander heaped upon him.

Blame, like death, is ready to descend at any moment. Unlike death, blame is not inevitable. As with praise, the mature person controls the blame he gives to others, if any. Too much praise, as too much blame, has ruined many a marriage. Too much praise as well as too much blame has spoiled life for many a child. When either comes your way, take it in stride. Neither is permanent! There is always tomorrow!

16. "LIVE AS ON A MOUNTAIN, FOR IT MAKES NO DIFFERENCE
WHETHER A MAN LIVES THERE OR HERE, IF HE LIVES AS
THE REAL MAN WAS MEANT TO LIVE."

It is said of the sages of the Academy of Jamnia (first century
A.D.) that they thus expressed their regard for all human beings,
learned and unlearned:

> I am a creature of God and so is my neighbor. He may prefer
> to labor in the country; I prefer a calling in the city. I rise early
> for my personal benefit; he rises early to advance his own inter-
> ests. If he does not seek to supplant me, I should be careful
> not to do aught to injure his business. Shall I imagine I am
> nearer to God because my profession advances the cause of
> learning and his does not? No! Whether we accomplish much
> good or little good, the Almighty will reward us in accordance
> with our righteous intentions.

Thus we live "as on a mountain," without its mattering whether
we live on a literal mountain or deep in a valley, so long as we
fulfill our own natures, so long as we "live as a real man was meant
to live," scholar or laborer, fisherman or physicist, butcher or sculp-
tor, or whatever else you wish.

Many a man lives "as on a mountain" and does not know it;
merit and fulfillment and maturity are often free of any sign of self-
consciousness.

You may remember Nathaniel Hawthorne's story, *The Great
Stone Face*. It tells of people who grew up in a small village amid
mountains; and all their lives they were aware of a great stone face
that nature had made visible on a high and distant crag. It seemed
a kindly face, forever sending wisdom, love, and peace down to the
village below. A legend had it that some day the village would
produce a man whose features were those of the great stone face.
The village did produce some famous men, who made careers and
fortunes in the outside world; but none of these, when they returned to the village in their maturity, could be seen to resemble
the great stone face.

Meanwhile a little boy named Ernest was born in the village and
lived there all his life. He was known for his wisdom, his compas-

sion, and his love for all of God's children. His Sunday afternoon talks were the highlight of the week. One Sunday afternoon, as he was speaking, the rays of the setting sun fell upon his face. The assembly was hushed and awed. Then a great shout arose: "Look, look, it is Ernest whose face is the great stone face!"

Thus the mature man is not self-conscious about the appearance he makes to the world; he knows he must build his maturity within himself. Without the frantic strivings of the money-mad and the fame-inflamed, he can show at last that he is the one among many who meets the highest standard. Hawthorne's symbol of this standard was the Great Stone Face.

17. "THE SOUL DOES VIOLENCE TO ITSELF WHEN IT TURNS
AWAY FROM ANY MAN OR EVEN MOVES TOWARD HIM
WITH THE INTENTION OF INJURING HIM, SUCH AS IN
THE SOULS OF THOSE WHO ARE ANGRY."

This book began with mention of two parallel stories from different parts of the great human storehouse of wisdom. Here again are two accounts from different sources that run side by side, as though each acknowledged the need to dramatize universal longings of the spirit.

The first, taken from Jewish folklore, is a legend of thirty-six righteous men whom God has placed upon this earth in order to save humankind from self-destruction. These men constantly come and go across the earth, performing good deeds. In appearance, they are as the lowliest of the lowly. You may deal with a humble, illiterate shoemaker or tailor; but by his kindness and humility you may suspect you are in the presence of one of the Thirty-Six. So one must treat with reverence any poor man, so long as he possesses goodness; and for that matter, any man, rich or poor, in whom goodness shows.

The Christian community has a similar legend: Once there was a poor shoemaker who dreamed that the Savior would visit his shop on Christmas Day. So, contrary to custom, early in the morning he opened his shop, cleaned it spic and span, and waited. There was no sign of the Savior. At last, in the afternoon, a little boy entered the shop to have his only pair of shoes repaired. He could pay only for heels, but the shoemaker gave him soles too. Then came an old woman in rags, begging for shoelaces, and the shoemaker gave her some. As twilight came, and the shoemaker was about to close his shop, a hungry beggar appeared and received some food. That was all.

Disappointed, the shoemaker went to bed. In his dreams, the Savior appeared. "Why did you not come to my shop as you promised?" the shoemaker asked.

"But I did come. I visited you three times. I was the little boy whose shoes you fixed. I was the old woman to whom you gave shoelaces. I was the beggar whom you fed. Even as you have done it for the least of my children, so have you done it for me."

It requires a high degree of maturity to realize that the helping of one's fellow man need not wait upon thirty-six righteous men. The Good Samaritan who does good for someone in distress or danger is primarily good to himself. Let him withhold his aid, however, and it is his own soul that he injures. This is borne out over and over again in human affairs.

One may sometimes refuse to heed a plea for help, since not every plea is worthy; and some pleas, if answered, may result in considerable damage to one's self. The mature person will listen, however, and will ask himself earnestly if he can and should grant a request. At the very least, he listens without anger; and he refuses, if he must, with no intent of injury in his heart.

18. "NEVER VALUE ANYTHING AS PROFITABLE TO THYSELF
WHICH SHALL COMPEL THEE TO BREAK THY PROMISE,
TO LOSE THY SELF-RESPECT, TO HATE ANY MAN, TO
SUSPECT OR CURSE, TO ACT THE HYPOCRITE, TO DESIRE
ANYTHING WHICH NEEDS WALLS OR GUARDIANS."

This time we will deal with two men—but they are very different men.

One was a man I knew some years ago who had a good deal of natural ability as well as an engaging personality. Everyone liked him, and he was climbing high on the ladder of success. When he attached himself to a popular and powerful politician, he soon climbed even higher. But then, in order to stay in his high post, he had to go along with his master's immoral methods. He participated in many of the corrupt acts that are so common—and so temporarily profitable—with dishonest people who gain power.

He and his boss were found out. They served prison terms. The man who had climbed so high came back to his community; he still had his wealth, his ability, his good looks, but he had lost his self-respect. He could never forgive himself. He could never rebuild the same life, even though, on the surface, all the same ingredients were there.

The other man was also a businessman of my acquaintance. I knew a good deal about his affairs and so I became aware that this man had turned down a potentially profitable deal because it was not quite ethical. It did not break any law, but still it was shady. When I asked him if he would tell me why he did not go through with the deal, and if he realized there would have been almost no chance of his being found out, he gave me a very significant and very mature reply: "Yes, I know. But if I had done it I wouldn't have been able to live with myself."

The mature man knows that what is most enduringly and satisfyingly profitable is to be able to live with one's self. To win the world's wealth and to lose one's self-respect is to be left with nothing but dust and ashes.

To desire that which requires walls and guardians is not in itself sinful or hurtful. One must look beyond the plain words. It is to allow such a desire to make you small and mean that is so damaging. Again, it is hardly possible to live through some decades without ever hating, pretending, or cursing; but where one's pattern of life allows only the merest occasional breath of such actions, no permanent harm will be done.

19. "BE LIKE THE PROMONTORY AGAINST WHICH THE WAVES CONTINUALLY BREAK BUT STANDS FIRM AND TAMES THE FURY OF THE WAVES AROUND IT."

The psalmist sang, "And who is a rock save our God." And, "The Lord liveth, blessed be my rock and exalted be the God of the Rock of my salvation."

The Bible speaks of God as man's rock of strength and refuge. And with that image in his mind, so can a mature man ground himself to a bedrock of confidence, courage, hope, and optimism. Waves of disappointment and trouble may batter him, yet there he stands. The stormy waters sweep over him, yet they cannot sweep him away. In truth, a man has a great advantage over a rock, for a man, if he is mature, has flexibility; he can give, sway, and ease the shock of circumstance. And when all may seem lost he still has his human mind to guide him.

There is a story of a painter who was unjustly cast into prison. He asked for paints so that he might follow his art even though denied his freedom. Paints too were denied to him. Now it would seem his life had no meaning; he had nothing to do but cast himself into a corner and weep in despair. This man, however, tore off a piece of his shirt. Then he bit his own arm to make the blood flow. Dipping the bit of cloth in the blood, he used it as a brush and painted pictures on the walls of his cell.

Many of us have heard the immortal lines: "I am the master of my fate, I am the captain of my soul." Here is the complete poem: *Invictus*, by William Ernest Henley:

> *Out of the night that covers me,*
> *Black as the pit from pole to pole,*
> *I thank whatever gods may be*
> *For my unconquerable soul.*
>
> *In the fell clutch of circumstance*
> *I have not winced nor cried aloud.*
> *Under the bludgeonings of chance*
> *My head is bloody, but unbowed.*
>
> *Beyond this place of wrath and tears*
> *Looms but the horror of the shade.*
> *And yet the measure of the years*
> *Finds, and shall find me, unafraid.*
>
> *It matters not how strait the gate,*
> *How charged with punishments the scroll,*
> *I am the master of my fate,*
> *I am the captain of my soul.*

20. "ON EVERY OCCASION I MUST ASK MYSELF THIS
QUESTION AND INQUIRE: WHAT HAVE I NOW IN THIS
PART OF ME WHICH THEY CALL THE RULING PRINCIPLE?
WHOSE SOUL HAVE I NOW—THAT OF A CHILD, OR OF A
YOUNG MAN, OR OF A FEEBLE YOUNG WOMAN, OR
OF A TYRANT, OR OF A DOMESTIC ANIMAL, OR OF A
WILD BEAST?"

Every man ought to examine himself carefully in regular sessions and isolate the quality of the maturity he portrays. Maturity is a becoming—a constant changing onto higher and higher levels of life-effectiveness. Marcus Aurelius, in his own way, knew this well. And he knew too that now and again we will slip back to the young-man or childhood stages of maturity; or worse, back to the rule of nothing but the savage instincts, as though one indeed had become a wild beast.

Maturity is a worthy handling of the circumstances of one's life —perhaps the "fell clutch of circumstance," as the poet puts it. Your record of maturity in the past does not guarantee mature actions now or in the future. What have you *now* as your "ruling principle"? Bring yourself up to date on yourself. Was whatever you did today worthy of that level of maturity that should be yours at your stage of life? Can you trace in whatever you did during the last week or month or year the burgeoning of maturity— the *becoming* of a human *being*?

Reading in the late Pope John XXIII's *Journal of a Soul*, I find that throughout his life, including his term as Pope, he was faithful to the practice of the daily confessional. He felt that by this regular checkup of his conduct, as well as of his conscience, he was able to keep his maturity in proper balance. For that reason, until his death in his eighties, his power of maturity was constantly growing active and effective.

He noted:

Practical experience has convinced me of this: The concept of holiness which I had formed and applied to myself was mistaken. In every one of my actions and in the little feelings of which I was immediately aware, I used to call to mind the

image of some saint whom I had set myself to imitate down
to the smallest particular, as a painter makes an exact copy of
a picture by Raphael. I used to say to myself: "In this case
St. Aloysius would have done so and so. He would not do this
or that." However, it turned out I was never able to achieve
what I had thought I could do and this worried me. The
method was wrong. From the saints I must take the substance,
not the accidents of their virtues. I am not St. Aloysius, nor
must I seek holiness in his particular way, but according to the
requirements of my own nature, my own character, and requirements of my life. I must not be the dry, bloodless repro-
duction of a model, however perfect. . . . If St. Aloysius had
been as I am, he would have become holy in a different way.

Note the striking resemblance to Zusya's thoughts and feelings
as legend reports them. Again and again the great truths of the
human spirit show themselves with different men and in different
ages; and yet they are eternally the same.

Chapter Six

YOU
AND THE INNER YOU—III

In preparation for the writing of this book, I put the question
"*What is maturity?*" to scores of people of differing backgrounds,
ages, and abilities. To encourage these people to enlarge upon their
answers, I also asked, "When does maturity come to a person, and
whence?" "How is maturity measured?" and "Can you ever be
sure you have attained maturity?"

Only two volunteered one of the fundamental theses of this
book, which had already become fixed in my mind, namely maturity is inborn. One person actually gave me the analogy of a plant
growing from its seed, an analogy with which I myself had started.
With most of the others I had to show good reason for my thesis
that the potential of a man's maturity is determined at birth. This
idea was accepted reluctantly. Skepticism was somewhat relieved,
however, by my assurance that the inborn potential (even in a retarded child) includes the capacity to develop one's maturity to
higher and higher levels.

Definitions of maturity were, in general, not very far apart. A
man in his late seventies said, "A person is mature when he has
lived long enough (this could be 20 or 220 years) and thought in-
tensely enough to be able to accept what people and the world do
to him; to accept these happenings and to react to them as crea-
tively, as cheerfully, and as charitably as may be within his power."

Another man, in his fifties, said, "Maturity is the capacity to
adjust to failure and defeat and to continue to work and hope and

succeed again. Maturity is a willingness to accept independence
and bear responsibility for one's own deeds. Maturity is the ability
to go beyond defeat, denial, despair; to face death honestly and yet
live hopefully and happily."

Still another, in his thirties, said: "Maturity means looking upon
defeat as a spur, not a sword. Maturity is bringing order out of
chaos; turning failure into success."

Out of the many opinions I had from the young and the old,
from men and from women, I would synthesize an "average" of
the definitions, as follows:

"The measure of a man's maturity is his readiness to accept the
bad in life and go on living beyond it toward the good; not to
grieve for the things he has not, but to rejoice in those he has."

And yet, although this is a true average insofar as words and
phrases can be averaged, it leaves out a good deal that was evoked
out of discussion. For example, most people agreed that maturity
also enables one to deal with success wisely; to handle the highs in
life as well as the lows with equal equanimity. Maturity recognizes
that joy can change instantly into sorrow. Maturity demands that
one balance fantasy with reality in proper proportion. Maturity
understands that nobody can be completely independent in human
society; that there are times when it is better to get than to give.

One day I realized that much of what we had adduced about
maturity could be found in a poem called *If*, by Rudyard Kipling.
I knew the poem, but I had dismissed it as being too corny. When
I reread it, valuing the quality of its thought rather than the quality
of its poesy, I found it to be rich and meaty with insight into what
it means to be mature.

Now that we have completed our especially wide front-view
mirror with twenty maxims from Marcus Aurelius, we shall add the
two side panels as we planned. One panel will be based upon that
very poem, *If*. The second panel will be made up of observations
on immaturity provided by an American business adviser, also as
planned. Thus, we shall have the three-way mirror complete before
this chapter is done.

Now here is *If*. If you have read it before, read it again.

IF

If you can keep your head when all about you
   Are losing theirs and blaming it on you;
If you can trust yourself when all men doubt you,
   But make allowance for their doubting too;
If you can wait and not be tired by waiting,
   Or, being lied about, don't deal in lies,
Or being hated don't give give way to hating,
   And yet don't look too good, nor talk too wise;

If you can dream—and not make dreams your master;
   If you can think—and not make thoughts your aim,
If you can meet with Triumph and Disaster
   And treat those two impostors just the same;
If you can bear to hear the truth you've spoken
   Twisted by knaves to make a trap for fools,
Or watch the things you gave your life to, broken,
   And stoop and build 'em up with worn-out tools;

If you can make one heap of all your winnings
   And risk it on one turn of pitch-and-toss,
And lose, and start again at your beginnings,
   And never breathe a word about your loss;
If you can force your heart and nerve and sinew
   To serve your turn long after they are gone,
And so hold on when there is nothing in you
   Except the Will which says to them: "Hold on!"

If you can talk with crowds and keep your virtue,
   Or walk with Kings—nor lose the common touch,
If neither foes nor loving friends can hurt you,
   If all men count with you, but none too much;
If you can fill the unforgiving minute
   With sixty seconds' worth of distance run,
Yours is the Earth and everything that's in it,
   And—which is more—you'll be a Man, my son!

One can hardly read this famous poem without seeing reflections of oneself. Let us now examine ten full-fledged maxims on maturity that *If* contains. These maxims and others to come will overlap some maxims that built our front-view mirror, but no part of a man's life can be held airtight and alone.

1. IF YOU CAN KEEP YOUR HEAD WHEN ALL ABOUT YOU ARE LOSING THEIRS AND BLAMING IT ON YOU.

When couples—and others—submit their quarrels to me, I often find that matters went from not-very-bad to bad to worse simply because someone did not "keep his cool." The phrase "keep your cool" is more modern than Kipling, but certainly its realization is timeless—that one lost head spreads its lostness to another and another. Thus it is when one person yells "Fire!" in a theater, panic takes hold, and many are crushed to death who otherwise might have walked away unharmed.

Let "blaming it on you" enter the picture, and we have a special source of emotional heat—for who likes to be blamed? As we have seen, however, children are almost incapable of accepting blame and so are grown-up children. If the blame is yours, you should accept it. If it is false blame, then eventually the truth will show. Meanwhile, the fiery retort and hair-trigger resentment do nothing but compound the mischief.

Each of us carries in his own mind special meanings of certain words and phrases—and special sensitivities keyed to our own special experience—which may have no deep meaning to another. Within this context you can see much room for misunderstanding. Maturity requires the calm recognition of this truth, rather than the flying-off-the-handle that ruins friendships, turns children against their parents, lights the fires of divorce: And all because there can be no complete communication; no real understanding.

I have learned, along with every other counselor, that it is well to have each party to a quarrel tell his story separately. You often find that a calm discussion, instead of hot anger, would have ended the quarrel almost before it began! More light and less heat is what most differences need. The mature person will give them that light no matter how much heat comes from others.

2. IF YOU CAN TRUST YOURSELF WHEN ALL MEN DOUBT YOU, BUT MAKE ALLOWANCE FOR THEIR DOUBTING TOO.

It was not easy or safe for such religious leaders as Amos and Isaiah and Jesus and Paul to state their principles and launch their campaigns of justice and brotherhood and love. In a world filled with cruelty and injustice, they could have gone right along with the Establishment. Yet, trusting themselves in the face of the scorn and doubt heaped upon them by others, they gave their messages to the world—and those messages never have been lost. Through them, their authors still live.

Science—the extension of human knowledge about the world and the universe—also has its heroes who faced disgrace and death, yet trusted themselves. Copernicus, Galileo, and Darwin dared— and received—ostracism, yet trusted themselves on the basis of their discoveries and studies. Inventors and technicians too have proved the "impossible" and still faced doubt and derision—as it was with the Wright brothers and their flying machine.

Read the life stories of such heroes and you will often find that they did more than dare the doubts of others. They were, at the same time, tolerant of those doubts. Maturely, they understood the long centuries of conditioning that may lie behind beliefs. They understood, too, that belief takes hold on a mass level, whereas advancement is made often by individuals who make great leaps ahead of the mass of mankind.

3. IF YOU CAN WAIT AND NOT BE TIRED BY WAITING . . . AND YET DON'T LOOK TOO GOOD, NOR TALK TOO WISE.

Again we are urged to cultivate the art of patience—an art attained by the highly mature. "I am tired of waiting" is an all-too-familiar phrase. It accounts for many a disastrous plunge into marriage when the disaster would have been visible if one had stopped and looked. It accounts for many a young man's stumbling and falling instead of going forward in his career, because—perhaps egged on by an immature wife—he presses too hard for a raise or changes his job too often.

"Don't look too good, nor talk too wise" adds a subtle touch. It is an admonition against acting superior when you have gained some advantage by waiting; an advantage lost by one who did not wait, or perhaps an advantage you forecast for yourself, so that now you say, "I told you so." It is an admonition against being forever in competition with others on a one-upmanship basis—which is never a mature approach.

4. . . . BEING LIED ABOUT, DON'T DEAL IN LIES, OR BEING HATED DON'T GIVE WAY TO HATING.

In short, do not stoop to the level on which your detractor or your despiser lives. Tit for tat does not eliminate the tat. Vengeance does not redress a wrong, but is more likely to intensify hostility, as in family feuds that go on forever.

Besides, if the lie or the hatred is unfounded, it will die of itself (unless your reputation is already so bad that any added damage is of little consequence). Bear in mind that lies and hatred directed at you do not change the real you unless you let them. The mature person will not permit that which is base and ugly to blacken his own soul. Otherwise, long after lies and hatreds are forgotten, one can find one's self still struggling to pull free from mud that clings to one because one was not proof against it, or to repair damage that still hurts because one gave it status when it came one's way.

5. IF YOU CAN DREAM—AND NOT MAKE DREAMS YOUR MASTER; IF YOU CAN THINK—AND NOT MAKE THOUGHTS YOUR AIM.

A legend tells that Adam was created so tall that his head touched the heavens. At the same time, however, his feet remained grounded to the earth. Thus it was made clear to man that while his thoughts and visions might soar far aloft, his feet should always remain on a solid foundation.

The dreamer not mastered by his dreams can turn a dream into a great reality, useful to himself and often to all mankind. The dreamer who is mastered by his dreams becomes a Don Quixote.

That well-meaning man, you will recall, dreamed great dreams of romance and knighthood, of chivalry and charity. These dreams mastered him so completely that he could not tell his dream world from the real world, and so, driven to reach for the unreachable star, to fight the unbeatable foe, the man of la Mancha left the high road and drove himself down the low road of absurdity and folly.

Thoughts and visions free the mind of barriers and open the way to very practical ends. In this respect, our dreams can be tools of maturity rather than an escapist end unto themselves.

6. IF YOU CAN MEET WITH TRIUMPH AND DISASTER AND TREAT THOSE TWO IMPOSTORS JUST THE SAME.

The late President John F. Kennedy once visited some troops who had been marshalled during the Cuban crisis in 1962. He told them he had come to thank them, because soldiers in peacetime rarely receive the thanks they are due. To make his point clear, he recited some lines scratched on a wall long ago by some unknown sentry:

> God and the soldier all men adore
> In time of danger and not before.
> When the danger is passed and all things righted,
> God is forgotten and the soldier is slighted.

Just so does the Man of the Year—deserving of his distinction at the time it is given—become the Forgotten Man in a little while. Triumph can be like Jonah's gourd "which came up in a night and perished in a night."

So it is with disaster, too; like triumph, it is fleeting. We are prone to make much of our failures and our successes, but notice how soon most of them dwindle out of sight. The mature man enjoys the moment's triumph yet takes for granted that one does not continue in an exalted euphoria. The mature man does not enjoy a disaster, but he learns from it and realizes that he need not remain downcast for long. Don't bore your friends with constant reminders of the highs and lows in your life. They have too many of their own. Rather, help them and help yourself to handle the circumstances and new becomings of life by constantly moving forward to the next and the next event.

7. IF YOU CAN FORCE YOUR HEART AND NERVE AND
SINEW TO SERVE YOUR TURN LONG AFTER THEY ARE
GONE, AND SO HOLD ON WHEN THERE IS NOTHING
IN YOU EXCEPT THE WILL WHICH SAYS TO THEM:
"HOLD ON!"

A few years ago an American bomber plane was discovered in the desert of northern Africa. During World War II, it had flown far off course after a mission, until it was out of gas and the crew bailed out.

The plane had crashed in a remote section and had remained undiscovered for more than fifteen years. Now the question arose: what had happened to the crew?

Eventually the bodies of those men were found in the desert. It seemed they had landed safely and had tried to walk to the sea. In the hot desert sun, with little water, they had never reached their goal. Yet they had walked twice as far as anyone thought could possibly have been traversed under those terrible conditions. Notes they left to be found with their bodies told of their thoughts of home and the families they had left behind them. It was nothing but will that, in each man's case, had forced "heart and nerve and sinew to . . . hold on when there is nothing . . . except the Will that says to them: 'Hold on!' "

Doctors speak of patients pulling through an illness after they were given up for dead—merely by the sheer will to live. Call it *will power* or *nerve power,* or call it *power of faith,* as I believe it should be called, and still you have a force that seems to transcend the physical. It is, perhaps, the ultimate difference between a man and a machine.

Thousands have lost races or have failed to gain some other successful end because they did not give their task that "something extra" that each of us has within himself. The Will that says "Hold on!" need not be confined to matters of life and death. In terms of maturity, it may be defined as that which keeps one going while any spark of hope remains. And if you should quit, then it will be clear that—like the lost airmen—you quit with honor.

8. IF YOU CAN TALK WITH CROWDS AND KEEP YOUR VIRTUE, OR WALK WITH KINGS—NOR LOSE THE COMMON TOUCH.

I have heard people say jokingly, "I don't think I would like it in heaven. It must be a lonely place. Most of the people I know probably will go to hell, so I'd rather join them down there."

Facetious as this is, it nevertheless points up the fact that most people generally follow the crowd. Alas, the crowd does too often "go to hell," in the sense that the majority spend more energy in yearning after vice than in pursuing virtue. The mature man thus stands apart in his very maturity. Never proudly aloof from his fellow men, he nevertheless does not descend to a crowd-level of unworthy thought or action.

What then is the common touch? It is the willingness to be numbered among the generality of mankind within one's basic opinion of one's self. Possessed of virtue, and not running with the crowd in its all-too-common pursuits, still one avoids the sin of pride. And so, when one walks with kings—if this should be one's circumstance—one nevertheless walks within one's own chosen approach to life—maturely.

9. IF NEITHER FOES NOR LOVING FRIENDS CAN HURT YOU, IF ALL MEN COUNT WITH YOU, BUT NONE TOO MUCH.

A wry old saying runs: "I can take care of my enemies, but please, God, protect me from my friends." This recognizes the fact that it is our friends and even our loved ones who, in a sense, can take an unfair advantage in affecting our lives. The out-and-out foe can be met with out-and-out resistance. The friend is first of all one whom you do not wish to offend. He may treat you with affection and admiration out of all proportion to your deserts. His blind

confidence in you—because he knows you're such a fine person—
may lull you into thinking you never can fail. Or, as we mentioned
before, a friend's all-out recommendation can go so far beyond
describing your real qualifications that it causes you nothing but
trouble.

A mature friend knows the power of ignoring an enemy; in business, for example, an unfair competitor can be allowed to go his
way while you go yours, confident that your continuing policy of
honesty, good service, and fair prices will win out in the end. But
a friend is not so easily ignored. He thinks he is helping you with
some advice, let us say, and if you do not follow his advice you
feel he may be insulted.

It is here that we see the wisdom of: "If all men count with you,
but none too much." Respecting the rights of all mankind, you
still do not surrender your essential *self*. This condition is sensed
and respected by others. In the end, it makes more friends, and the
best kind of friends.

It is interesting to note that *If* was a favorite poem of Mahatma
Gandhi. Surely there was a man who walked with kings yet never
lost the common touch.

10. IF YOU CAN FILL THE UNFORGIVING MINUTE WITH SIXTY SECONDS' WORTH OF DISTANCE RUN.

What is "distance run"? In one case it may be work. In another
case, with the same person, it may be play. Many of us never find
out that play sometimes is the best "work," and so, in the end, our
achievement level suffers.

Kipling's message in these lines is: Use the irreplaceable
moments of your life for purposes that are good for you and for all
that makes up your life and your vista of human relations. Use the
minute—unforgiving because, once wasted, it never returns to be
lived again—to *live* in a worthy manner. Let every minute find you
the best person you can be at that stage of your life.

Now we are ready to set up our other side mirror. This one, you will recall, is to deal with *im*maturity. By showing us an unpleasing picture, it will encourage us to make a beautiful picture out of our lives. And this time we go to a living person, Dr. Robert N. McMurry, and to advice contained in his manual *How to Recruit and Select and Place Salesmen.*

Dr. McMurry has already been introduced as the head of a top-rated personnel counseling agency. He has spent many years in the business of analyzing and evaluating the capacity and competence of men—for positions ranging from stockboy to company president.

Long ago, Dr. McMurray learned that not only salesmen, but also directors, managers, superintendents—in fact, anybody in any job—must be mature in order to function effectively. Out of a wealth of observation and experience, of study and survey, he has distilled the major immaturities—the ever-present enemies who constantly raise their ugly heads. Here are ten of his delineations of immature action and attitude. With them we shall build the final panel of the three-way mirror that shows us ourselves.

It is immature:

1. TO SEEK AND USE MONEY OR MATERIAL THINGS AS ENDS IN THEMSELVES—NOT MERELY AS MEANS TOWARD THOSE ENDS.

Many a candidate for a sales position or other job makes it clear that his interest in a job revolves around one factor, *money.* Betraying selfishness at a childish level, his only basic question is, "What's in this for me?" He does not seek to present what he can *give* to the company. Such a man often is an "angle boy" who boasts of his own cleverness and regales you with stories of how he manipulated others with whom he did business. Obviously he has no scruples about exploiting anyone, including his employer.

There is nothing wrong in asking for money for your services. It is wrong, however, to give the pursuit of money a rating of top priority; to make it the ruling passion of your life.

Remember King Midas. All he wanted was gold. He wished that everything he touched would turn into gold. His wish was granted.

But when the food he was about to eat turned into gold, and when he touched his own dear daughter and *she* turned into gold, the lesson became all too clear.

Neither your food nor your daughter will turn into gold; but anyone to whom money is an end, not a means, still lives on an immature level. In fact, he misses much that is good in life because he "turns it into gold"—he chooses a standard that has no breath or warmth, the *gold standard*. Money buys much for us that is needed and enjoyable, but when it buys your soul, you sell your soul.

2. TO ACCORD PLEASURE UNDUE IMPORTANCE.

A child is naturally pleasure-minded. Left to his own he will eat without restraint, play without measure, and wish to be endlessly entertained. Only later comes the ability to distinguish between a fleeting and perhaps harmful pleasure and the state of genuine happiness. It comes, that is, if a person really grows up!

Since most of us rarely, if ever, face starvation or bitter exposure to the elements, we rarely think, as our ancestors did, in terms of avoiding physical disaster. We tend more to think of ways in which to increase our pleasure, and that hardly takes any thought at all. For the immature, the pursuit of pleasure is a careless, automatic process. Only the mature man takes the long view of life. It is he who asks of himself: "Is this good for me or bad for me?" Or more particularly: "On the basis of true life-happiness, shall I indulge in having this food or this drink, this sex experience or this cigarette?" This is not a puritanical viewpoint that denies pleasure as a valid part of life. It is, rather, a balancing of the short- and long-term views of living.

A typical "salesman" situation gives a good case in point. Notoriously, salesmen spend many hours at movies and double-headers when they should be working. Not being under the eye of a boss, they neither get to work on time nor attend well to their work, no matter what may be the ultimate consequences.

One day the sales manager calls a salesman's home to leave a message with his wife. It is, say, 11 A.M., so the sales manager assumes the salesman made his first business call two hours ago. But to his consternation, the wife says cheerfully, "That's all right, Mr. Jones, I won't have to take a message. George is still at home."

Nor does the gradually shortening work-day seem to satisfy the widespread desire to avoid work. Even business conferences must be held over cocktails in a fine restaurant, to the sound of night-club music. Vacations become stretched, more elaborate—and hard work in themselves. When the accent is forever upon pleasure for pleasure's sake, this is immaturity.

3. TO LIVE ONLY FOR THE IMMEDIATE PRESENT.

Allied to the preceding criterion, this one inevitably reminds us of the fable of the grasshopper and the ant. The grasshopper chirped and fiddled his way through all the warm plenty of summer. The ant, meanwhile, toiled to gather food and store it against the time when the ground would be barren and cold. When winter came, the ant lived well. The grasshopper was reduced to misery and beggary. See the grasshopper as symbolic of the immature!

Remember, too, the Biblical story of Pharaoh's dream. The ruler of ancient Egypt dreamed he saw seven fat cows and seven fat ears of corn; then came seven lean cows and seven lean ears of corn that swallowed up the fat ones. Joseph, Pharaoh's adviser, interpreted the dream: the fat kine and corn represented seven years of plenty that would be followed—as indicated by the lean kine and corn—by seven years of famine. Joseph warned Pharaoh not to allow his people to gorge themselves on the produce of the fat years, but to store extra grain in huge granaries against the demands of the lean years to come. Thus, when the days of famine arrived, Egypt was able to feed its own people and neighboring people as well.

Thus we have yet another of those themes of wisdom that run through both ancient and modern lore. *The mature do not live merely for the present* is a lesson of timeless strength.

4. TO COMMIT YOURSELF TO A WORLD OF FANTASY.

Dr. McMurry reminds us: "Many children live lives rich in fantasy, as is well known. But what is not well known is the fact that this trait is also characteristic of numerous adults."

Normally, anyone may engage in a certain amount of wishful thinking. The habit can grow, however, till it becomes both wasteful and harmful, and even a definite hazard in that it interferes in one's dealings with the here and now.

A stage play, *Joe Egg*, revolves around a couple's efforts to handle the problems posed by a spastic child. The child is also practically a vegetable from the standpoint of mental and emotional reaction. In a television interview I heard the play's star, Albert Finney, explain that the drama is bearable for its audience because its rich humor provides escape from the grim theme. In this sense, humor is a kind of realistic fantasy that relieves many a tense and sad situation. And hope is a realistic fantasy that can deliver one from despair. And so is faith. I mean the faith that is born in man as set forth in my book, *The Power of Faith*. Such faith is not blind. Anything that takes you away, even for a little while, from some bitterness into a better world that perhaps one day may be, serves you well. Fantasy is sometimes man's only safety valve when he feels he is drowning in reality's vale of tears.

But recognize fantasy for what it is—a creation of the mind, useful indeed, yet not real. A mature person lets fantasy extend his vision, but never allows it to becloud his view of what is real.

5. TO BEHAVE AS IF YOU WERE ALL-POWERFUL.

Psychologists agree that, in infancy, the child tends to become the center of much attention. Most children learn when very young that if they cry or throw a tantrum they can have almost anything they desire.

Carried on into adult life, this feeling is no longer a reality but a believed fantasy. The adult still believes that if he demands something strongly enough, he will get it. Often, his parents have given him such omnipotence in his childhood that he cannot do without it; he is more comfortable in not letting himself grow up.

Another aspect of such immaturity lies in an inability to see another person's viewpoint. This often leads to a life of bickering, unhappy marriage, and hostility in everything one does. Or, if it lifts a person to a position of power, the position becomes completely insecure, for such a person in high office surrounds himself with enemies.

Obviously this holdover from infancy is an immature attitude.

6. TO BE A SHOW-OFF.

Do you generally boast of your achievements and possessions? Are you a conversation-grabber? Must you be the life of the party? Then you have a carry-over from your childhood, when you were the center of attention, and you still want to have your ego massaged.

Are you a hypochondriac, or do you have a hypochondriac within your range of observation? Then observe (if you are capable of standing off and looking at yourself) that hypochondriacs are basically show-offs. They are out to draw sympathy and attention.

For example, as your family doctor can tell you, there are many mothers who decide to have "heart attacks" when a bachelor son wants to marry and cut the spiritual umbilical cord. Mother thus puts her own well-being in a position of extreme drama—and she will do it as many times as she can. To show off with a purpose is only a more expert kind of showing off.

People show off in the same manner—with fancied or exaggerated disabilities displayed for attention—in order to avoid all sorts of situations they consider unpleasant. One such situation often is *work*. Showing off is a symptom of both immaturity and insecurity. Watch others—or watch yourself—and you will see.

7. TO HAVE NO SELF-CONTROL.

Here too the child remains visible in the behavior of the adult— to the adult's cost and society's. Ordinarily, a child proceeds gradually in learning more and more self-control—control of his appetite, control of his bodily functions, control of his temper, control of his innate selfishness that is merely not understanding that others have rights too. This self-control comes along with the or-

derly development of maturity. Self-control is taken for granted—
when one is old enough to think about it—as one of the qualities
that makes it possible to live in a give-and-take world.

And yet how many adults one meets who have never developed
an effective "thermostat" to govern their wants, their temper, and
their general relations with others. It is obvious that once such an
immaturity is rooted in a person it is most difficult to remove. The
worker who has temper tantrums will go on finding it a hard job
to hold a job. The executive who has a bad temper will find he is
not in control of his authority. And the parent who *blows up* may
rear a child who has acquired the same habit—a damaging immaturity, and always a handicap in handling the situations of life.

8. TO DODGE THE ACCEPTANCE OF BLAME.

We have touched upon this immaturity before. It is interesting
to note that it becomes a significant factor in the realm of business,
too. Grown-ups take exactly the same stance taken by children.
"I didn't start the fight with my brother" merely becomes "I didn't
snarl at the customer." "I don't know who broke the TV" becomes "I don't know who had the car when the fender got crum-
pled." "My sister made me (do this or that)" becomes "My
husband—wife—boss—made me. . . ." And so on.

McMurry calls such adults "alibi experts." They never make
mistakes. They can do no wrong. At the most, they will claim
they have been misled. In this area we find great ingenuity. For
example, someone who has blabbed a confidential statement will
defend with the excuse: "But you didn't say I couldn't tell it." Or,
if the other person had asked for secrecy, the alibi expert still will
find a way out. "But I didn't know I was supposed to keep it secret
all my life," he will say.

If you deny blame often enough, you may be sure that even an
absolutely true excuse is no longer convincing. Be mature enough
to accept blame if you deserve it. This is not *Mea culpa*—"I am
guilty"—in the sense that you find a reason to blame yourself for
everything that goes wrong, for that in itself is an immaturity. The
mature person can say factually, "I was wrong," or "It was my

fault," and not feel that he has destroyed his inner worth. Others know this too. In fact, anything you know about your own maturity or immaturity is quite certain to be known to others.

9. TO BECOME TOO DEPENDENT UPON INDEPENDENCE.

Some of the saddest cases of emotional immaturity are those who never have been able to divest themselves of the swaddling clothes of dependence. No matter how old they may be, they must run to Papa or Mama for guidance, or find someone who will take their parents' place.

Against these, Dr. McMurry calls attention to the over-strivers. They have a compulsive need to prove their independence by denying their dependence—any degree of dependence upon anyone else. I know men who would be much more successful if they consulted with others. Executives, especially, often make the mistake of not letting others have a voice in decisions. They not only lose the benefit of getting someone else's viewpoint, but also they do not allow others to develop their own executive skills.

These over-strivers often end up as under-achievers. This occurs when, at last, they cannot hide that they are weak, not strong; dependent instead of independent; plagued by insecurity and blocked by immaturity. To depend upon another person—the right person—at the right time is to show a mature understanding of the interaction of minds and abilities. As we have said before, no man is self-made.

10. TO BE A MISTAKE-BLOTTER.

A bachelor has been defined as a man who never has made the same mistake even once. As a joke this is all right; but note how it borrows from a very serious matter—the tendency of human beings to repeat their mistakes again and yet again.

A fool has been defined as one who will not learn from his mistakes. If so, then there are many fools who have high intelligence. What does the damage is an immature attitude, mistake-blotting, the blotting-out of the mistake as a valuable experience. One therefore remains neither changed nor instructed, but quite ready, willing, and able to commit the same mistake again.

Mature people make mistakes, but their mistakes become profitable investments. The mature mind sets up a warning sign of caution along some action-road or emotion-road on which an accident has occurred. This being accomplished, there is one less wrong turn to take in life. One has grown: one has, by virtue of having made a mistake, become all the more capable of dealing well with circumstance.

This completes our three-way mirror. The front panel is especially wide, like the new wide cinema screens, so that you may the more effectively face yourself. The two side panels work with the front panel to let you view yourself from many angles.

Stand often within the three-way mirror. Read the forty maxims; grow with them and their meaning will grow with you.

Maturity and a good marriage walk hand in hand. Immaturity and marriage, alas, were not made for each other. Let us look at maturity (and immaturity) in relation to the wedded state.

Chapter Seven

YOU AND YOUR SPOUSE

In a little town far back in the hills, a woman came to court seeking a divorce. Since everybody knew everybody else, the judge was quite shocked to see her.

"Why, Miranda," he said, "I just can't believe it. You and Tom have always seemed such a happily married couple. After forty-five years of being together, what in the world makes you want to separate from Tom?"

"Well, Judge," came the grim reply, "the trouble with Tom is that in the last ten years he's been behaving more like a husband and less like a friend."

We hear over and over that husband and wife must be companions, must be lovers, must be partners in life. True. And before and after all these, they must live together as friends. Friendship, indeed, makes up for much that never may be achieved or quite perfected in companionship, in love, or in partnership. We can see quite plainly what Miranda meant when she said, "more like a husband and less like a friend."

Whence comes the friendship that blesses a good marriage? It begins with two individuals who are essentially strangers. The husband and wife may, before marriage, have lived close to each other and they may have "gone around" with each other since childhood. But they come from different families and influences and find—as they never really noticed before—that their personalities and purposes are quite far apart.

The great majority of new couples have been attracted to each other by that mysterious magnet called love. Some, of course, were drawn together by just money or status, or driven together by only pity or despair. But even in the truest love-match, the two, embraced and absorbed in their deep feeling toward each other, in many ways remain separate and different from each other. What then can assure a happy marriage for a man and a woman who have two separate minds, two separate sets of conditionings, and two different ways of looking at life? It is the power of maturity that both bridges the gaps and holds the two together. Not love, strong as it may be, but maturity is the bond that makes a happy marriage.

Delightful as the story of Moses Mendelssohn and his Frumtje may be, and wonderful as their love was, those two, with their maturity, made their marriage right here on earth. During their period of courtship the two young people, to some extent, enter a world of fantasy. A honeymoon and the first few weeks or months of marriage also may proceed "up there on Cloud Nine." Eventually, however, the differences between man and wife—in heredity, in background, and in so many other areas—show through the rosy haze. There comes a time when the two must recognize that they are human beings. Nobody ever married an angel.

How then shall they build strong pillars, solid walls, and firm floors in their house of maturity, in that relationship called Marriage? Let us examine the matter in the light of three stages that make a good marriage. These stages begin long before the marriage, with wooing. The second stage is winning, where so many stories end, still in the rosy never-never land of "They lived happily ever after." The third stage is welding, the triumph of maturity in marriage, when "happily ever after" really can be made to work.

1. WOOING

There is much truth in the facetious remark that the male pursues the female till she catches him. And once a girl discerns that interested gleam in the eye of a boy she likes, she feels encouraged to continue the chase.

George Ade tells a story about two girls who lived in handsome houses on the same block. Each was quite beautiful, they were of the same age, and each was intelligent, well educated, articulate, and otherwise attractive. Girl A was so popular that every evening her front porch was crowded with young men eager for a date. Girl B, on the other hand, sat alone in her porch swing, enviously watching all the excitement across the street.

What was the difference? Beautiful and eligible Girl B, who sat all alone, had had a few dates. But she would spend the entire evening talking about herself—*her* ideas, *her* hopes, *her* achievements, *her* expectations. The result was that her date was bored and never came back. Beautiful and eligible Girl A, however, understood that the way to make anyone like you is to show an interest in that person. She made her young men feel that she was deeply interested in *them; their* ideas, *their* hopes, *their* achievements, *their* expectations.

A mature young man, responding to such advances, will not talk long about himself before he begins to draw out the girl in the same manner. Thus two people really get to know each other, and find out how "I" and "You"— which never disappear—can also form a valid "We" in marriage.

It is no new discovery, however, that, in the late teens and early twenties, the major spur of love is not reason or attraction, but strong emotion. Sexual drives are at their most urgent. "Making out" is a status smybol. Thus the would-be-married of either sex becomes vulnerable to various subtle, screened maneuvers.

Despairing parents have compelled me now and again to "play God" in breaking up prospective marriages. I have felt justified in doing this only when I could see there was a woeful absence of maturity.

I remember a college student who had been helped in his studies by a very brilliant girl who was singularly unattractive in ways more than skin deep. What the young man thought was love was really gratitude.

Then there was the boy in his early twenties, pursuing a degree in law, who became sexually trapped by an exotic nymphomaniac. There was the young man preparing for a business career who married only because he was intrigued by the wealth of his sweetheart's family and the promise of a high position in the company her father owned. There was the girl, a college senior, highly attractive at twenty-two, who was ready to marry a blatantly unsatisfactory suitor because she was afraid of becoming an old maid. In each case, reason gave a forbidding *"No"* while other forces clamored for a *"Yes."* A bit of insight, a touch of maturity developed in quiet discussion, and a mistaken marriage was averted.

On the other hand, I once used legal pressure to force a bachelor in his forties to follow through into marriage with a spinster of thirty to whom he had become publicly engaged. On the promise of marriage she had given up her teaching position and had already been given engagement parties and showers. Moreover, they seemed highly compatible, and he admitted he was just as fond of her as ever. But he had allowed some money-hungry sisters-in-law and his old father, with whom he lived, to convince him that he was making a mistake. Under the threat of a breach of promise suit, this man married the woman who wore his ring. It became a very happy marriage.

2. WINNING

Engagement may be considered either as part of wooing or as a definite winning. Surely something depends upon how seriously one accepts the engaged state. Let us consider, however, that when the young man pops the question and the girl's "Yes" is spoken, she is won.

What is really won? Nothing but a consent to marriage. One might say that a battle has been won, but not the war. Often, the victory defeats itself.

In fact, engagement at times acts as a great letdown. The young man, now accepted as one of the girl's family, hears certain remarks and sees certain actions that do not please him. He realizes that, until he was "hooked," the family had put on its company manners when he was around. All this can apply to the girl too.

The engaged couple themselves tend to discard their company manners. The great lover now may let something slip that shows he is a gross liar. The sweet young thing, now feeling free to speak her real mind, may turn out to be a gold digger who uses a sharp spade. On top of all this, the parents of the groom, once glamorous, perhaps, may now be seen as utter bores or those of the bride as misers. Then there is the parade of relatives and friends whom one must accept as members of the wedding. Then—and these require maturity to handle—come many other questions: What kind of honeymoon to spend, and how much to spend on it; where to live; what kind of home will suit both parties; are children desired soon, and if not, when, and how many; what interests can be shared and who should give up what; who simply cannot stand whose best friend; and so forth, and so forth.

It is at the "winning" stage—engagement—that these and many other questions may arise, seemingly out of nowhere. But of course they were there all the time, hiding behind the pink clouds of wooing. Suddenly it appears that the boy's income is not really sufficient; and, after all, the girl's father cannot subsidize him. Or the widower, now blatantly showing that he expects gratitude for marrying her, wants the lonely widow's savings to support them in style while he treats himself to an early retirement. The "winning" stage, then, is a winning stage only when maturity has first been won on both sides. With maturity come honesty and insight, and the ability to handle problems and meet on common ground. Or, more likely, two mature people will never become engaged to marry if there is any reason why their marriage would be a mistake.

3. WELDING

A fellow clergyman once told me that he had jokingly offered the following advice to break the tension that often attends a wedding. "When I have pronounced you man and wife," he said to the groom, "you slap your bride. When she asks, as she brushes the tears from her eyes, 'Darling, what was that for?' you tenderly answer, 'Dearest, that was for nothing. Now start something.' "

Such a scene is hardly likely to occur. Yet often I have thought what a blessing it would be if both bride and groom were struck with a hard blow of reality, to make sure they knew that the task of making a marriage begins as soon as the ceremony ends. It continues especially through the entire dream world of the honeymoon, while the real world is still far away. It never completely stops, for there is always the need for maturity in making two into one—yet never quite one.

Again, when a marriage ceremony is over, I have observed the same letting down that so often comes with a formal engagement. No sooner have a couple been pronounced man and wife than they begin to unmask. So do their parents. One hears and sees much that was guarded against during the wooing period, and even during the winning period. The wedding reception goes on with great gaiety; there is fine food and wine and dancing; but, alas, the ghost of failure is dancing too.

Let us look at some statistics. Marriage authorities W. T. Ogburn and M. T. Nimkoff have found that 26.5 per cent of all divorces in the United States were granted to couples who had been married for two years or less. When one considers that the conditions that create a divorce generally go on for some time before man or wife reaches the final hard decision, and that the legal steps also take time, it is a fair assumption that most of those marriages did not really last more than a year.

The same authorities found out that 51.3 per cent of all U.S. divorces were granted within the first five years of marriage. This too indicates the wide prevalence of marriage ties that begin to rub raw and become frayed and thin in the early years of marriage.

The Institute of Life Insurance has made a careful study of the incidence of divorce and the time of its occurrence. They conclude that the younger the bride, the greater the chance that the marriage will fail. When both bride and groom are in their teens, the chances that the marriage will fail are twice as great as they are when the bride is over twenty-one and the groom over twenty-four.

Experienced marriage counselors bear witness also to the fact that marriage is best undertaken by mature people. We have seen that maturity does not depend directly upon one's age, but, among the young, there is undoubtedly less willingness to work at welding and perfecting a marriage.

In most marriages, the differences and difficulties that arise between husband and wife are generally of a minor nature. As a rule, any quarrel that arises can be resolved by two normal and reasonable people who are prepared to give a little and take a little. The union of the marriage is then like welded steel in that it will bend and so save itself from breaking. But marriage cannot withstand continuous bickering and backbiting, nagging and deceiving, which, like a continuous hammering, can break the bond.

Many a couple has found it advisable to set up some safety valve or escape hatch that goes into action when a quarrel is ready to erupt. There is a point to the humorous story of a husband and wife who were increasingly annoying each other until they decided to give each other the final say in certain fields. The husband was to have priority in all major matters; the wife in all minor ones. He could sound off as he wished about Civil Rights, Viet Nam, taxes, and so forth, and she would merely listen. She would decide how to handle the children, where to go on vacations, and such matters—and he would accept her decisions.

There is also the story of the seventy-five-year-old man who went to his doctor for a check-up. The doctor looked him over and exclaimed, "Why, you have the body of a man thirty years your junior! How do you keep yourself in such wonderful shape?"

"Well," said the healthy oldster, "When my wife and I were married, more than fifty years ago, we agreed we would never have an argument. If we saw an argument coming, and it involved a minor decision, my wife was to take a walk around the block, cool off, and accept my judgment. If it involved a major decision, I was the one who was to take a walk around the block, cool off, and accept *her* judgment. And to this system I owe my present health."

"You mean," said the doctor, "that you have in this way been able to keep your peace of mind?"

"No," said the oldster, "it's because I have taken so many walks every day that I have lived an essentially outdoor existence."

Marriage is always a union of two *people*—never of two *saints*. If either man or wife expects the other to be perfect, or considers himself or herself to be perfect, a large shadow of immaturity hovers over them. Also, for either to expect the other to be the same kind of person is an immature attitude. Bearing these matters in mind, let us now set forth Ten Rules for Maturity in Marriage. Try them on for size, so to speak, as you view yourself in the three-way mirror.

1. YOU MUST WORK AT YOUR MARRIAGE.

You must work at your marriage both to give it life and to keep it vigorous. Divorce is not the only thing that will kill a marriage.

Indifference will kill a marriage. Neglect will kill a marriage. Drifting apart and separating in interests and associations will kill a marriage. I once came across the story of a childless couple whose marriage had been in a state of living death for many years. Nevertheless, for reasons convincing to themselves, they wished to avoid a legal separation. Instead, for years they went their separate ways, maintaining separate bedrooms, eating breakfast and lunch separately and engaging in separate activities during the day. If they met at the dinner table or for social engagements, it was generally in the presence of friends. They avoided being alone with each other.

One day, the husband, who was a very prominent citizen, learned from some friends that his wife had written a book which was becoming a literary success. He read it and discovered it was autobiographical. Its contents contained a suspicion of scandal. It told of the author's heartbreak in the loss of a man with whom she had lived many years ago and who now was gone forever. The date of her deep interest in this man with whom she had lived as revealed in the book was after they had been married. The husband angrily confronted his wife and charged her with adultery. He demanded to know the name of her secret lover. For a long time she refused to tell him. At length, she cried: "You were that man. You were once the wonderful idealistic young man whom I loved and adored. But that man died long ago. Now all I have left is the man he became—one whom I know to be selfish, mean and a cheat, one whom I can no longer love or respect."

A mature man knows that his wedding ceremony is only a contract. The ring he slips onto his bride's finger is only a symbol. What counts is how the contract is kept. What matters is the gold of character, not the gold of the ring. Both parties must work at making a marriage work—even in the middle years of a marriage— even in its twilight days.

I know too many couples who obtained a divorce after their children were grown. I officiate at too many funerals of very old people who have been separated for many years from their spouses. The story is usually the same. At some time in the course of the marriage one party or both stopped working at it. And strangely enough, as a noted divorce lawyer reports, 90 per cent of divorced persons who remarry choose the same type of person with whom "they could not get along" before. The first marriage could not have been all wrong, then. But the interest was lost. Or someone saw greener pastures—he thought—which really were quite the same as his own.

2. WORK FIRST ON YOURSELF.

During World War II, it is said, President Franklin D. Roosevelt nightly uttered an old Chinese prayer: "Reform thy world, O Lord, beginning with me."

Most of us take the opposite view. We'd greatly prefer to have the world changed to suit us. I know that as a rule I find husbands and wives are much more concerned about getting their spouses to change than in effecting changes in themselves. Typically, they complain about the stubborn refusal of their mates to control certain habits, attitudes, and mannerisms that they had before they were married. Regarding themselves and their own built-in habits and attitudes, however, they can see only that such aspects of personality are necessary parts of their being. They may insist that some of these traits are part of their own charm—part of "the real me." It never occurs to them that their mates feel the same way about themselves.

Often I have heard women say, "I'll change him after we're married. I know he's stingy and stubborn sometimes, and he'd rather not have anything to do with music or books, which I love. He's all business. But he does love me, so he'll let me show him the values to be found in a different way of life. . . ." And so forth. Compromise can be reached; both husband and wife can give a little; but the only road that can lead to any change in one's spouse must begin with a willingness to change one's self.

3. INFLUENCE YOUR SPOUSE BY BUILDING HIM UP.

If you'd like to read a fine play about the way a wife helps fashion her husband's success, read James Barrie's *What Every Woman Knows*. The wife, in this play, gives the husband priceless behind-the-scenes guidance but also lets him think he has managed his success by himself.

Not every wife can come up with great ideas to be planted subtly in her husband's mind. Any wife, however, can soften the blows of her husband's work and keep on building him up with praise and encouragement. Even when talking to a man about his disappointments, a wife can give him new courage and hope. She can make him important—if not in the business world—then at least in his own home. At a recent funeral I heard a bereaved husband say with tears in his eyes, "She made me feel like a king."

The husband and breadwinner needs encouragement—but so does the woman who stays home and keeps the house. If the labor of many a housewife were to be truly evaluated, she might find she should be paid a higher salary than her husband's. A mature man in a mature marriage will let his wife know that he does not take her cooking, cleaning, caring for the children, shopping, and sewing for granted. He will let his wife see that he notices and appreciates the contribution she makes to the marriage they share.

With human beings, as with human affairs, it is easy to find fault. Search diligently rather for something you can honestly praise. Make your spouse know that he or she *counts* in your life. The best work is done and the best lives are lived by people who do not feel they are nameless ciphers.

4. COMMUNICATE WITH YOUR SPOUSE.

The same lawyer I quoted above declares that a large number of divorces are due to lack of communication. Love in marriage or friendship can be shunted aside by a misunderstanding or misinterpretation. Maturely, good communication steps in and the hurt love or friendship is cemented again. Too often, however, immature resentment, pride, stubbornness keeps the line of communication broken. Later it's "Why didn't he tell me?" But later may be too late.

In *Your First Year of Marriage*, the marriage counselor Tom McGinnis points out that communication is carried on with more than the voice. Mind can reach mind with the wink of an eye, the shake or nod of a head, the shrug of a shoulder—and mates whose minds and hearts are attuned to each other will understand. Mr. McGinnis says that "communication in marriage is keeping in touch with each other so that each of you knows what's going on inside."

Obviously that favorite weapon of the immature, the silent treatment, is not the right kind of communication. Nor is an angry voice or a scornful look. Nor the slamming of a door, nor the throwing of a dish. Sometimes one cannot avoid the silent treatment, but in such a case let your spouse know what is on your mind and don't let silence last long. Anger and scorn, too, may at times be unavoidable—but get done with them quickly.

When I was in college, I sold books from door to door to earn some money. Being still young, I was amazed to find that many housewives revealed so readily their lack of communication with their husbands. Sometimes they had not spoken to each other for years. Husbands gave their wives an allowance, but never gave of themselves. Wives served meals—along with a heavy, silent serving of contempt. I am older now and no longer so amazed; but I am always saddened when I find couples who do not communicate and so have ruined what might have been a good marriage.

5. TELL YOUR SPOUSE OF YOUR LOVE.

Tevyeh, the central character of *Fiddler on The Roof*, asks his wife, "Do you love me?" She hardly understands what he means. She points out—in song—that for twenty-five years she has cooked for him, washed his clothes, borne him children, cleaned his house, and nursed him when he was sick. Now why must he ask whether she loves him? She cannot understand that all he wants from her are those three magic words, "I love you."

It is, in fact, difficult for many wives and husbands to say those words once marriage is past the honeymoon stage. Before, the words came easily; now they trip up the tongue. Women especially want to be told they are loved. Women are more aware than men that the world is full of their rivals; and, of course, women often stay home while men go out among other women who may be younger, prettier, more desirable. A man may bring home flowers or jewelry or a fur coat—he may show his appreciation of his wife and tell her as much—and yet she wants those words "I love you."

The longer the period that goes by without those words being spoken, the harder it becomes to say them. The wife becomes inhibited, afraid to mention what is so precious to her. The husband, perhaps, feels it is not quite masculine to "get emotional." Yet there is a strong, real need for more than gestures and caresses of love in marriage. The verbalization is important. It is a reassurance that the original flame of love—the flame that welded the marriage—still burns between heart and heart.

Byron put it well in a few lines of a long poem, *Don Juan*. A woman is speaking:

> Man's love is of man's life a thing apart;
> 'Tis woman's whole existence. Man may range

The court, camp, church, the vessel and the mart;
Sword, gown, gain, glory offer in exchange
Dress, fame, ambition to fill up his heart.
Men have all these resources, we but one—
To love again, and be again undone.

6. BE TOGETHER WITH YOUR SPOUSE.

"Togetherness" was a popular term a few years ago. Perhaps too many jokes were made about it, since it is rarely used today. It is meaningful, however, and important as a concept.

Bear in mind that living together does not automatically mean *being* together. There is a basic togetherness that, like marriage itself, needs work by both parties to keep it strong. It is a mistake for husband and wife to sleep in separate rooms, and even a mistake to sleep in separate beds in the same room. (Of course, illness or some other special reason may require it.) The closer a couple stay physically, the closer they stay in mind and heart. It is well known that when two people sleep in the same bed over a period of years, there is less chance of separation or divorce.

Husband and wife should attempt, if at all possible, to go to sleep and arise at the same time, and even to put out their reading lights at the same time. They ought to have breakfast together, too, and make the day's first meal a prime time for communication. Having lunch together is often not practicable, but dinner should be had together, and most often at home, the shrine of the marriage.

A mature couple will also find ways to develop common interests, the husband joining the wife in some of her favorite occupations and the wife joining the husband in some of his. They should have the same friends, too; not "your friends" and "my friends."

Nor should children ever be made to feel that either their mother or their father is more important than the other in their lives. Most of all, they should be given no opportunity to play off one against the other. As for husband and wife, neither should attempt to play off his or her parents against the other set of in-laws. In true mature togetherness, there is no jealousy and no favoritism in this area. If, as sometimes happens, in-laws interfere in a marriage, then husband and wife should for a time let them be out-laws no matter whose parents they may be.

Togetherness is all-embracing. There is no part of a marriage into which it does not reach. Find it and you armor your marriage against adversity.

7. ALWAYS AND FOREVER BE FAITHFUL TO YOUR SPOUSE.

It is well known that infidelity is one of the most frequent causes of divorce. Almost anything else can be forgiven and forgotten; unfaithfulness leaves an unhealed wound. Even the suspicion of unfaithfulness rankles bitterly. A wife knows that if her husband's work takes him traveling, he may be lonely and looking for entertainment in some strange town when his day's work is done. And she knows that women are easily available if a man wants them.

Or again, a husband cannot leave his work, so a woman goes alone or with some female friend for a trip abroad. She misses her husband, is lonely without him. She reasons that she is entitled to have a little fun. And so at a bar or at a dance or on a promenade deck or a beach, a man speaks to her and she is flattered. Or perhaps her female friend meets some man and that man has a friend and—what's the harm, after all? Soon the "harmless" flirtation goes too far. When the woman sees her husband again she feels sick and shamed. True, he may never know; that is, unless her friend, who talks a lot, whispers it around as a "secret." But even if the husband never finds out what went on in the hotel in Marseilles, the wife never will forget. And never stop wishing it had not happened.

Nor do matters have to go very far. Flirting is always dangerous. It is never entirely innocent; it implies too much. I know of one attractive woman who bet another woman that she could make a very prominent man take her to lunch. She won her bet, and the man lost his wife. I know of another woman who was seen sitting in a man's lap, and that was all—but it was too much. She was divorced after twenty-five years of marriage.

There is no room in marriage for even the suspicion of unfaithfulness; nor even an unfaithful thought. A mature person will take care never to imply, however indirectly, that he possibly could consider being unfaithful to his mate.

8. TRY HARD TO FORGIVE YOUR SPOUSE.

Infidelity leaves an unhealed scar. Yet, even if he or she is unfaithful, *try* to forgive your spouse. The trying itself is felt, and is good. Make quite clear the significance and consequences of such an act to your marriage. Let the straying spouse know that his (or her) image has been flawed, that your relationship has been strained, and that such strayings remain forever on the record. At the same time make clear that your love that helped build the marriage is mature and great enough to endure.

For the sake of your love, forgive. You cannot forget, but time will thrust the event into the background of your life. Marriage exists on many levels. There still is room for it to be strong and joyous.

Hurts and wrongs in marriage are more likely to be smaller but repeated. There is the thoughtless word carelessly spoken; you read into it a hidden criticism and make something permanent of it when it was only a passing mood with the other party. Or, a birthday or anniversary is forgotten, and you feel that *you* have been forgotten. Or your wife has bought some expensive clothes when *you* know your money is so tight you can't afford a new suit. Or you come to the conclusion that your wife is a poor housekeeper— or your husband has no appreciation of the work that goes into housekeeping. Or he spoils the children, or she nags the children too much. . . .

Whatever it may be, do not see it as a push-button signal to complain and condemn. Try to understand the other person and that other set of motives that is part of your marriage. Have you allowed for the occasional careless word from your spouse that you would expect him to forgive if *you* said it? Might it not be a good idea to set up some mutual reminder system for birthdays and anniversaries? Have you ever really sat down with your wife and explained your finances? Is your wife aware that good housekeeping can be learned? Are you conscious of what really goes on in the minds of your children?

Then there is the matter of a spouse's habits that you know are bad, or that "drive you crazy." Intemperate, inflammatory condemnation will not end overeating or chain-smoking or excessive drinking. Sometimes you may need the counsel of a psychiatrist. In many cases, however, working patiently with a spouse will disclose that he is anxious to end his damage to himself, and when he knows he has your cooperation, he can do it.

Forgiveness comes first, then a change for the better. Forgiveness opens the lines of communication that resentment closes. Forgiveness also removes the fear of resentment, or even the fear of punishment that can stand as a barrier of reconciliation. Forgiveness, maturely offered, can never come too early after a conflict develops. As a rule, it is never too late.

9. WATCH YOUR LANGUAGE WHEN YOU TALK TO YOUR SPOUSE.

One of the most frequent statements made to me by wives who seek my counsel when they are considering a divorce runs like this: "You wouldn't believe the kind of vicious language my husband flings at me. I'd be ashamed to repeat what he calls me."

Words can be sharper than knives. Words that hurt need not be unrepeatable. Husbands, for example, complain about the constant barrage of ladylike—but definite—abuse with which they are bombarded from the moment they come home from work. Everything they do seems to be wrong. Everything they fail to do is linked with some sinister reason; for example, a wife will refuse to believe that her husband might have forgotten to buy something she needed because he was beset with serious business problems. She'd rather believe he was busy with another woman.

Many women do not realize what a weapon they have in their sharp tongues. A man's only answer may be to knock his wife across the room—but few men, fortunately, will do that. A man can feel peculiarly helpless against a stream of constant nagging, an avalanche of unrelenting, nasty talk-talk-talk beating on his head. When he is at length enraged into action, the wife may not understand how she has provoked him into going out with a slam of the door that shakes the pictures off the walls.

Some women learn at last. A wife confessed to me recently that she was facing her second divorce only because she was too fond of continuously questioning and nagging her husband. You can talk yourself out of a good marriage. And you can do it all the faster if you do it in public. Many a marriage has been destroyed by a few words that would have passed practically unnoticed if said in the privacy of the home—but which were disastrous when said over a bridge table or after a few drinks at a party.

10. TREAT YOUR SPOUSE AS AN EQUAL.

"Spouse" in this case generally means "wife." An ancient sage said that if your wife is lower than you, you should stoop down to bring her up to your level; if she is higher than you, reach up and stand by her side on the same plane. He meant that in marriage there is no place for the terms *inferior* and *superior*. Each spouse should think of the other as having special gifts and qualities that are poured into the marriage for the benefit of both; that both are not exactly the same should be regarded as a blessing and not a burden.

Men are stronger than women, taller than women, and it is true that women tend to get tied down with their babies. But are women of a lesser breed than men? Not at all!

Recently, in New York City, a new breed of feminists formed an organization called NOW. The acronym stands for the National Organization of Women, which demands "full equality for women in America in truly equal partnership with men." It threatens to picket with a prominent display of signs. These women argue that women are valued not for their intelligence and other similar qualities but only for their sexuality—that is, "as wives and mothers, which, stripping the matter of its traditional sacred cows, reduces the woman's role to a sort of socially acceptable whoredom."

Unfortunately, their extreme position is not without a basis in fact. Too many husbands automatically assume that their wives are inferior in understanding and in various other matters that "should be left to men." Allowances are doled out to wives as though they had no understanding of the value of money, when as a matter of fact their understanding tends to equal or exceed men's. Or such phrases as 'A woman's place is in the home" are built into vast systems for enslaving women. Nor is it true that women are more emotional than men, though they may show their emotions more openly. Nor is it true that women are less intelligent than men— although men may have more chance to learn and display specific skills.

Someone said: "Married people create their own worst problem —children." People of mature outlook know how shallow a remark this is. Children are usually a marriage's greatest blessing, but they need to be reared with the same mature outlook that makes so much difference in every part of life. Let us look into this very important aspect of maturity.

Chapter Eight

YOU AND YOUR CHILD

Of all the stories I could tell you about parents and children, this one is my favorite.

A wealthy man provided his family with all the comforts and luxuries that money can buy. Since he and his wife were busy with their social and business schedules, he made sure that their little boy and girl had a nurse and also a governess. The governess could have the use of a car and a chauffeur to take the children anywhere. If the children stayed home, they had every kind of toy and game to keep them happy, and a big swimming pool besides. The father, when he saw his children now and then, beamed upon them and urged them to ask him for anything they wanted.

Then came a business reversal. The father went broke. Gone were the nurse and the governess and the chauffeur. The family had to move into a modest apartment. With no money so spend on entertaining and socializing, the parents had to stay home a great deal. This did not seem so bad since the whole family could be together. One night, parents and children were having a wonderful time, singing and laughing. Suddenly the little girl, seated on her father's lap, looked up at him fondly and said, "Daddy, please don't ever be rich again."

A very significant story! I as a counselor—and any judge or lawyer who deals in family matters—can tell you how true to life it is. When one hears a parent say despairingly, "I gave my boy (or girl) *everything*," and that boy or girl is always in trouble, you know the parent did not give everything. Just as the little girl in the story instinctively knew, there is no substitute in a child's life for a parent's attention, interest, and constant love.

Some people, physically parents, never really seem to be able to learn what parenthood is all about. It requires a muti-faceted maturity. There is a great giving of one's self. And there is a great need for perspective as regards your child—for he is at one time both an extension of yourself and a separate human *becoming* who must not be hindered in his increasing need to be himself.

Some people simply do not want to be parents. There was a female robin—as the fable goes—who built the most beautiful nest that the bird kingdom had ever seen. Dozens of birds flew all around the nest, admiring the way in which Mrs. Robin had intertwined the twigs and interlaced the leaves.

Then a fussy little wren hopped onto the edge of the nest and peered down inside. "Mrs. Robin!" said the wren, "why in the world have you left a big round hole in the bottom of your nest?"

"Oh, that?" said Mrs. Robin. "So simple! I adore building nests. I love laying eggs. But I hate kids!"

Thus it is in many a beautiful home where no children ever arrive. The factors that make a couple—or at least a woman—not have children, when she could have them, are many and deep. We need not go further here than to mention that the anti-child feeling may be rooted in childhood inhibitions and so in some form of fear. Let us go on to consider the average couple. They do have a child or children. And they often find themselves "out on a limb" with a commitment that, once assumed, cannot be given up. Sometimes parents think they hate their children. I say "think" they do, because they really don't. But thinking that way is bad enough.

Anxieties about children, however, come to practically every parent. The parent never sheds them completely; rare is the great-grandparent who is not still anxious about his children, although they are now grandparents in their own right! Parents might as well resign themselves to being at least a little anxious over their children's welfare; they can laugh at themselves, and so help to hold the tendency in check.

Real trouble starts when anxiety turns into antagonism toward the child. It is one thing for a mother to worry because her daughter is not pretty; another entirely for the mother of a homely daughter to demand of the world, "Why must I put up all my life with this ugly duckling who never will catch a man!" Let the daughter hear this—and she will—and she will lose all confidence in herself.

It is one thing for a father to worry about his son, who is below average mentally; another for him to say, or even show in his attitude toward the boy, "Why was I afflicted with such a stupid oaf?" Whatever learning power and maturity power the boy has can be badly inhibited by this kind of damnation.

I have noticed, too, that the parents who most resent a retarded or ungovernably "bad" child are often the parents who have done the least for their child. Most such problems become evident in the very early years. Immature parents, however, refuse to deal with the grim reality of the child's condition in time. They rationalize and temporize; they grow angry at the suggestion that their child may have a fault; they must wait and see. Yet the sooner these problems are given professional attention, the more hope there is that something can be done.

Often, the case of a disturbed child can be traced back to roots far outside the child's own mind. Some years ago in our temple we supported a child-guidance center for the community. The director's basic theory was that a disturbed child is the product of a disturbed family. His therapy for the child, therefore, was group therapy. It consisted essentially of questioning the child in the presence of various members of the family and thus confronting all of them with a problem common to all, and for which all were responsible. In talking the problem through from several angles, and gradually pinpointing its specific familial roots, he was often able to find a way of relief. When the parents were helped, the child was helped.

A distinguished child heart specialist states that most mothers of afflicted children are worse problems than the condition itself; and that very often the mother is the primary cause of the affliction. There are psychologists who assert that children's feeding-time problems (the terror-time of many a mother and child) are either caused or aggravated by their mothers. Army psychiatrists report that in a high percentage of non-physical rejections, the major reason is some disturbance arising out of family background. A day-care-center director asserts that emotionally starved children are the products of emotionally starved parents. Where can the cycle be broken?

Perhaps, in the future, we shall not need to be concerned about the normality of our children. A startling report from a recent science conference, *Humanoids to Order*, deals with a series of stunning breakthroughs in the field of genetics. The study suggests that even nonphysical factors such as intelligence and personality —and, I would add, maturity—are more dependent upon heredity than we have hitherto imagined.

Experiments revealed that: "Working with a bacterium, a one-celled creature . . . researchers have devised means of altering its genetic code in favor of some specific trait and then having the genetically engineered bacterium pass on its new traits to its off-spring. For example, a gene that permits one bacterium to be resistant to a certain chemical that kills other bacteria can be transmitted to different types of bacteria to make them resistant also."

Now, a human egg begins as a one-celled structure. These same scientists are convinced they can actually change the genetic code of a human egg. This presents the prospect of a couple's being able to order the traits they wish for their children. Blue eyes? Blond hair? High intelligence? Athletic stature? We may be able to name it and get it! And if not by actually tinkering with the human egg, then with another suggested technique—the injection of a pregnant woman with viruses freighted with whatever new genetic information she may wish to have transmitted to her unborn child.

Other scientists are skeptical. Professor Francis H. C. Crick of Cambridge University, a Nobel Prize winner and co-developer of the modern theory of the genetic code, said that the prospect of improving the human race by altering its genes was unlikely. He insisted that education and environment are more important than one's genetic background.

Some day we may know the answer. Meanwhile the parent-child

relationship remains about where it always has been. For some time, particularly during the recent "pal" period, we have stressed the importance of a parent's personal attention to and association with a child. Rightly, we have pointed out that all the money and education and privileges a parent may give a child cannot take the place of his actual physical presence and friendly concern. Yet the child must still be helped to become a mature person in his own right, not a dependent of the parent. The Syrian poet Kahlil Gibran said it well:

> You may give them your love, but not your
> Thoughts, for they have their own thoughts.
> You may house their bodies but not their souls,
> For their souls dwell in the house of tomorrow
> Which you cannot visit even in your dreams.
> You may strive to be like them, but seek not
> To make them like you,
> For life is not backward nor tarries with yesterday.
> You are the bows from which your children as living
>   arrows are sent forth.

Now, what makes a mature parent? (Please note I have not said a "perfect" or a "good" or a "wise" parent. There is no such thing as a perfect parent any more than there is a perfect person.) Well, a mature parent is first of all human! He need not be wise, yet he can learn and follow the rules of maturity. He does not even have to be good, in the general sense, in order to be a mature parent. I know many parents who are good for their children, but who themselves are far from being "good." Goodness helps and innate wisdom helps, but neither is absolutely essential in the development of maturity in children.

Bearing this in mind, read, ponder and remember these Ten Basic Rules for Maturity in your relationship with your child:

1. YOU MUST KNOW YOUR CHILD AS HE REALLY IS— AND THEN ACCEPT HIM FOR WHAT HE IS.

It requires no courage to accept a healthy, normal child, especially if the child is bright. But to accept a child as he really is when he is crippled, when he is spastic, when he is subnormal in any way—this is a different matter. And different again—terribly different—when a child is almost two people. Many a child is highly intelligent, gifted in one or several ways—but the victim of paranoid schizophrenia. His seizures turn him into a demon. His condition is practically incurable. Yet parents live with such children, accept them for what they are, and gradually make their peace with the sad reality. Now there is a ray of hope, since schizophrenia seems to have been traced to hematological factors, but it may take some time before a cure or a means of relief is narrowed down.

I have known many parents of mentally and emotionally retarded children and I wonder at their fortitude—the smiles on their faces and their kindness and patience with their own child and with all others. Among such parents I know one extraordinary couple who both have achieved success in their professions. Their first child was entirely normal; their second, a year younger, is mentally retarded. Both children live at home. Maturely, the parents attempt to give the older child as much attention as the younger, so that he will not feel neglected. And the family goes on.

The genius child can be another kind of problem. I have seen parents make the mistake of treating a young genius as though he were a god; or perhaps a fragile piece of china that must not be subjected to the daily wear and tear of ordinary use. Before long the child was controlling everyone else in the family.

The genius child is still a child. When the genius grows up he may resent the way his parents handled him. He may be genius enough to know that he is spoiled and selfish, and that he has his parents to thank for it.

2. ACT UPON WHAT YOU KNOW ABOUT YOUR CHILD.

In a day-care center, it was found that it was much more difficult to aid a four-year-old than his three-year-old brother. Both suffered from insecurity, but the younger could be "reached" far more easily; help had come at an earlier age. Once you spot trouble, don't listen to friends who assure you that time will heal. Sometimes it does; but assume yours is the exceptional case. The shame that parents should feel lies not in having an ill or retarded child, but in not having done anything about it.

Not so many years ago, parents such as Pearl Buck and other sensitive and intelligent people reluctantly brought their retarded children to institutions to be cared for. It was assumed that the retarded child never could be equipped to function in the outside world. Now, as I have mentioned earlier, we are finding ways to help many retarded children attain a certain degree of maturity. The spark or seed is always there. Work with it, and you may find a retarded person performing certain jobs better than many normal persons can.

The younger the child is when the parent *acts* toward helping him, the more can be done for him in most cases. Recently, I visited a group of children and teenagers whose I.Q.'s ranged from 50 to 70. Some were physically handicapped as well as being emotionally disturbed. Even so, they appeared to be active, alert, interested, and happy. They were learning the three R's—readin', 'ritin', and 'rithmetic. But they were also acquiring the discipline of three more R's: routine, repetition, and relaxation. The older ones spent half the day on tasks such as gardening, cooking, laundering, carpentry, brick-laying, and serving in the dining room. Thus they developed skills and thus each one developed a sense of individual worth. Even one child of very low intelligence, engaged in peeling potatoes, had a concept of the whole: he saw himself as feeding the entire school.

Such children can put on plays and learn to play music. It is amazing how much latent ability cannot be determined by Binet scales or Rorschach tests. Year by year we find out better ways to help retarded children develop into useful members of society. Act for your child, then, when he lags behind the others. Act promptly. The sooner you act, the more chance you give him to lead a life he will enjoy.

3. LOVE AND CARE FOR YOUR CHILD.

I spoke to the director of a day-care center, who confirmed what so many others have said.

"A parent must really love and care for a child," she said. "The fundamental love may be there, but a parent must show love so that the child can experience it. Just how? Well, we fondle and coo to our babies and make a fuss over them, but also, every mother should try to breast feed her baby. If a bottle must be used, then the mother herself should hold that bottle. A baby can tell! And the father should hold the baby, and occasionally change the baby, too. Personal attentions are more valuable to the child than are amusing toys. The baby should be aware of the giver, not only of the gift."

As she talked, there flashed into my mind the story of the wealthy man who gave his children everything except himself—and how his daughter, that "poor little rich girl," was happy that poverty now kept her father at home. How many busy, prosperous parents never realize that a child must be fed emotionally as well as physically, must be given love, which is more important than toys and games.

Genuine love—not an anxious possession—does not spoil a child. The mature parent knows the difference. And a father never should think that loving and caring for children is a mother's job alone. The father who is too blusteringly masculine to be bothered with household matters, or too busy with his work and his lodge, is neglecting an essential task. Parents should share the care of their children as much as they can. The reward can be priceless and life-long in bringing emotional security and maturity for the child.

4. BE HONEST WITH YOUR CHILD.

I am a person who believes that it is wise to be honest with our children, and in our Temple when our teachers at our religious school present the stories of the early patriarchs, of Moses and the exodus from Egypt and the giving of the Torah on Mt. Sinai, they are expected to say that these are stories handed down to us by our ancestors; that we have faith in them, but that we cannot prove they are true any more than we can absolutely prove the existence of God himself. Thus we establish for the child a foundation of truth upon which we can build a religion made up of reason as well as emotion, of logic as well as faith. We do not create a credibility gap that may vitiate all our later teaching.

We tell fairy tales to children and we present them as fairy tales. They are still enjoyed without bearing even the possibility of truth. Along these lines, I should like to see Santa Claus given the same treatment. When the child discovers that Santa Claus is only a fiction, he may wonder as to the validity of other statements from his parents that are given to him as facts. The gifts and joy still can be there. And children can understand from the start that the extent of the gifts depends upon their parents' prosperity far more than it does upon "being good." There are too many good children whose parents are too poor to have Santa Claus bring expensive presents.

Be especially sure not to lie to your child about himself. If he says to you that he is not so smart as Johnny, do not insist he is. If he obviously is not, let him know that he doesn't have to be. Tell him the plain truth—that we all are born with widely varying capacities and abilities and interests. And again, that what a person lacks in quick comprehension he often can make up by hard work, dedication, and concentration.

Be honest as well with the daughter whose mirror tells her she is not as physically attractive as some other girls. Help her to improve her physical appearance—there are so many ways, these days. Even more important, show her how to become more attractive through the mature use of heart and mind and spirit. When you think she is ready to understand, tell her this: A woman cannot be blamed for not being beautiful before she is twenty-one; but after that age she is at fault if an inner spiritual beauty does not shine through her eyes and glow softly upon her face. Help her find that kind of beauty by finding maturity. It is a beauty that is visible at seventy-one, too.

Above all, be honest with your child by never asking him to do what you would not do. Often I tell parents that I sympathize with a child in our religious school who balks at attending worship services. When he says, "Why should I go when my father and mother say it's good for me but they never go themselves?" I am on the child's side.

5. GUIDE YOUR CHILD.

I have a friend whose five-year-old son showed some talent for music and the piano. He was started on a regular schedule of instruction and seemed to enjoy it. A few years later, however, baseball became his obsession. It became increasingly difficult to keep him at the piano for the daily practice that good playing demands.

One afternoon his father took him, as he often did, to see a big-league game. As they were leaving Wrigley Field, the boy began to complain, "Aw, Dad, why do I have to do that piano practicing when we get home? What I need is pitching practice."

The father, a sensible man, had long been aware of his son's growing distaste for the piano. The mother had been just as aware. But they knew, too, that a parent should advise but not always decide. And they were mature enough not to have to fulfill themselves in their child's glory—that is, by force-feeding him with some talent or profession not truly his.

Still, the father made one last try. "You know, son, many people can play the piano, but you are one of those who will be able to play really well. Don't you want to have that personal joy, and also be able to give delight to others?"

"Yes, I know," said the boy helplessly. Children do not have the resources to come up with the other side of such arguments. "But I . . . but . . ." And he lapsed into silence and looked back longingly at the ball park.

"All right," said his father, "you're through with the piano and your mother and I are through with struggling to make you practice. So you won't be a great concert artist!"

The boy, his mother, and his father got along much better after that. But there is an interesting sequel. Later on, when home on vacation from college, the young man was found practicing on the piano for hours. The parents heard clumsy attempts at composing and saw signs of frustration.

One evening their son asked in an agonized manner, "Why did you let me stop taking piano lessons?"

"Well," said his father, "we got tired of pushing you and hearing you complain. Music was not so vital that we felt we had to make it our decision instead of yours."

"You should have made me! Now I'll never be a good player!"

"Ah!" said his father, exchanging a glance with his mother, "if we had forced you to practice the piano instead of playing baseball, you might now be complaining to a psychiatrist about us!"

There may be no "piano trouble" in your home, nor anything that corresponds to it. The important thing in all cases is to give your child the benefit of your knowledge and experience, but not to impose your will on his. (Some exception must be made for going to school and doing homework, and a few other basic matters.) After he is old enough to think for himself, however, increasingly let him decide on what he will choose to keep out of all that life offers him, and what he will cast away. You will still be guiding him—but play your guiding lines as a driver plays a spirited horse, never holding him so tightly that his spirit is broken. Let the child occasionally go racing forward on his own wild adventure, and he may appreciate you all the more, and turn to you for guidance because you do not force it upon him. Don't be too concerned if your child disowns most of the beliefs you hold as long as he does not disown you.

6. DON'T BE AFRAID OF YOUR CHILD.

There still are areas in which a parent must see to it that a child does what is expected of him. I have seen parents terrorized by five- and six-year-old tyrants who refuse to listen to any form of reason, and from whom affection brings no response. There are the little "angels" who won't stay in bed no matter what the hour, who won't take their medicines, who won't allow their elders to carry on a conversation, and who will slap and kick their parents. And smilingly indulgently, the parents will remark that their children show a great deal of spirit, and protest little or not at all when a ten-year-old insists on staying up for the late late show.

About a generation ago, parents and children became victims of an extreme permissiveness. It became something close to a crime for a parent to deny a child anything. But we have changed our ways, and with good reason. Some psychologists now teach that spanking is an acceptable form of therapy, and that at the proper time it is the only kind of language that can put the message across —to the child's benefit.

Do not spank for spanking's sake. It may help to recall the old story about the farmer who claimed he never had to beat his mule. Just a loud command, a "Giddyap!" would get the beast to move along obediently, he said. One day the farmer wanted to drive his wagon through a shallow stream, but the mule balked. The farmer shouted several "Giddyaps" but the mule would not put his hoofs into the water. Finally the farmer picked up a stick and hit the mule as hard as he could. It moved. The farmer then remarked to a bystander: "I never beat this mule. I just use a stick to help him remember."

Boys and girls really prefer rules of discipline if those rules follow two rules in themselves. First, the discipline must make sense. Second, it should be reasonably and justly enforced. Children respect a parent they can trust—and trusting includes the knowledge that disciplining will be handed out if the occasion warrants.

7. DON'T BE OVERDEMANDING.

If you really know your child, his weaknesses, and his strengths, you will not demand of him more than his maturity potential can produce. You will help him become—not like Moses—but like Zusya, that is, his best self.

Remember that it is more important for your child to be happy within himself than for you to be happy with him. If your son decides to be a house painter, don't drive him into distraction by insisting he should be a portrait painter. If he wants to go into business, don't try to heckle him into studying for a profession.

While he is still young, remember that, at five or six or a little older, children are not ready to be ladies and gentlemen. It is less important for them to keep their clothes clean than for them to have fun with their playmates and express their normal exuberant feelings.

You may not enjoy having your child get poor marks in school. You may enjoy even less the smug smile your neighbor gives you because *his* child gets straight A's. If your child is working at his full capacity, you may harm him by demanding more. Find out, of course, if he needs the attention of your family doctor or a psychologically trained adviser. If he is functioning normally and trying honestly, however, let him just make passing grades if he can. Find your own parental satisfaction in his lovableness or his charm. Some of the dearest children I know are not the smartest; and some of the brightest children are not the best kind of children to have around the house.

"For the childrens' sake," many a family strains to live at a higher level than they can really afford. Or they push children into private schools that demand too much of them, hoping that they thus will meet the "right people." Push your child around and you gain his resentment and often his open rebellion. Drive him too far and you will drive him away.

8. DON'T EXPECT GRATITUDE.

The motion picture *Guess Who's Coming to Dinner* has a dramatic scene in which a Negro father tries to dissuade his gifted and successful son from marrying a white girl. The father reminds the son of his own hard work as a mailman, slogging through the mud and snow for all the years before his retirement. He tells the son how both his parents denied themselves a great deal in order to send him through college. In short, the father tries to control a child's actions by presenting a bill for a debt of gratitude. And the child—of course he is an adult now—flashes back, "Dad, I owe you nothing."

This truth, so bitter to immature parents, has been recognized for a long, long time. A very wise woman, Glückel of Hameln, lived in Hamburg toward the end of the seventeenth century. Widowed and left with several small children, she worked day and night so that they might survive. Her *Memoirs* tell:

"We should, I say, put ourselves to great pains for our children. For on this the world is built, yet we must understand that if chil-

dren did as much for their parents, the children would quickly tire
of it." She follows with a parable:

> A wise bird once set out to cross a windy sea with three
> fledglings. The father bird had to carry his young across the
> water, one by one, in his strong claws. Halfway across, he said
> to the first fledgling, "My child, you see how I am struggling
> to save your life. When you are grown up, will you provide for
> me in my old age?" The fledgling replied, "Only bring me to
> safety and when you are old I will keep you in the greatest
> comfort." "You lie," said the father bird, and dropped the
> fledgling into the sea. He then went back for the second
> fledgling, and over the stormy waters he asked this young bird
> the same question, and received the assurance "I will care for
> you in your old age and give you everything you wish." "You,
> too, are a liar," said the father bird, and dropped the second
> fledgling. He returned for the third fledgling, carried him out
> over the sea and asked the same question. This one replied:
> "Father, I hope I shall be able to keep you in peace and honor
> when you are old, but I cannot bind myself. I can promise,
> however, that when I have grown up and have children of my
> own, I shall do as much for them as you have done for me." At
> last hearing the truth, the father bird carried the one truthful
> fledgling to safety.

There is no use in saying that a child *should* feel gratitude
toward his parents for bringing him into the world, taking care of
him, perhaps sacrificing much for his sake. Only an immature
parent will wield "gratitude" as a ploy for winning the child's
obedience or for forcing him to think as the parent thinks. The
mature parent will be delighted if gratitude is expressed, but not
dismayed if never a word of gratitude is spoken.

It has been said that one father can support ten children, but ten
children cannot support one father. It is well known that many a
young married couple lives with or is supported by one set of parents for some years; but later, when those same parents are old, the
younger couple will contribute little or nothing toward their support. Are the younger couple, then, giving freely of their resources
to their own children? One always hopes so. One cannot always
know.

Whatever may be your own situatoin with your children, do not make the mistake of expecting gratitude. And do not make the worse mistake of using gratitude as a weapon. It is a feeble weapon indeed, for something in human nature makes sure it is of no avail.

9. DON'T BE OVERPROTECTIVE.

Now and then, when I talk with parents, I ask, "If you were able to bring up your children all over again, would you follow the same methods you used before?"

Most parents say they would manage somewhat differently. Very often they say that they have come to realize they were overprotective of their children. They intervened too often to save them from hurts, failures, and sorrows. Only later did they see that the inevitable bruises of childhood—both mental and physical—are all part of the maturing process.

Sam Levenson, a comedian who once was a teacher, tells how his mother treated him when, as a child, he was sent home because of some disciplinary problem in school. She would slap him and haul him back to school by the ear. She made him beg the teacher to forgive him and please give him another chance. Today, however, a mother is more likely to accuse the teacher of not knowing how to handle children, and to threaten to bring charges against the teacher if her child is "picked on" again.

It is rare that a child has to be protected against a teacher. Most such interference by parents fails to protect the child's best interests —that is, the development of his own best self. Even if the teacher does make a mistake, the child learns that one can suffer through the mistakes of others. He learns that those in authority are not always right. He learns lessons of life he needs to know when his parents will not be there to present his case.

Don't fight your children's battles for them. Don't do their homework for them. Don't protect your child from his own deliberate failures—the consequences of his not doing homework, for example, or the consequences of his being antagonistic to his friends. If he is allowed to stumble a few times when he is young, he will know all the better, later on, how to walk strong and straight.

10. PRAISE YOUR CHILD.

Most babies get a lot of loving. Still, there are times when it must seem to the child a few months old that he is in terrible distress and has been left alone to suffer. He is hungry, he howls—and has to wait and wait to be fed. He is uncomfortable, he howls —but nobody runs to change him. He would like to be picked up and appreciated, but nobody seems to care.

The baby still has it easy compared to the child of walking age. Suddenly he is not permitted to eat this or drink that. He is expected to pay some attention to his clothing. He has to learn that strange new discipline called toilet training. And a little later he has to go to school, which deprives him of many hours of play. All this time he is finding out innumerable ways in which he can get himself scolded or punished.

Worse yet, he finds out there is injustice in the world. He may be punished or at least admonished for something he did not do. Typical of the approach of the average parent to the average child is the story of the mother who is preparing dinner while her child is playing in an upstairs room. She listens to the noise he makes. When he is quiet for a moment she shouts, "George, whatever you're doing up there, stop it!"

The child, then, grows up in a world full of ways to do wrong. What can the parent do, even while "civilizing" the child, to make that child feel there is nothing really wrong with *him* and that the world is not such a bad place after all?

A large part of the answer lies in giving the child love. Another closely allied secret lies in praising him, directly and indirectly. Even children who function well without praise will blossom more fully under its warm radiance. Certainly, a child who does not possess the normal share of maturity requires a good measure of praise. The more a child seems prone to fail in achievement, compared to other children, the more he needs praise and recognition for what he does accomplish.

Unfortunately, most parents are far more ready to blame than to praise. They take a good performance as a kind of respite from the bad. Yet a child, just like an adult, will respond to an image of himself that is set up for him. When you show a child that you always confidently expect him to act in a praiseworthy manner, he is likely to do so.

One of the many tales about Sam Goldwyn tells about his performance on the golf course. Apparently he was generally so poor a golfer that he expected to go on being a duffer. On this occasion, he took a mashie shot about 125 yards from the green. After the ball struck the ground, it seemed to disappear. Both Goldwyn and his caddie searched for it. Finally, the caddie looked into the cup— and there was the ball! Goldwyn was bewildered. "What did I do that was right?" he muttered. "What did I do that was *right?*"

Goldwyn, of course, was a success in other directions. A child, however, leads a more circumscribed life. Any failure can be felt through his entire life-pattern. In the course of events, any child will fail now and then to accomplish some task or to meet some standard. His general view of himself, however, depends a great deal on how his parents interpret his failures. Are they signs of his bedrock character—and so, must he go on through life never expecting to do anything right; expecting failure and getting it? Or are his failures mere incidents, experience from which he learns; small stumbles that only temporarily interfere on the path of success? The parents' attitude can make the difference. Praise can be the vehicle for giving the child confidence in himself.

No matter how "hopeless" a child may seem, look deep into his personality and his performance. Talk about the one "B" mark he received, not the three "C's"; about the one good companion he has, not the three doubtful ones; about the fine job he did in cleaning up his room instead of about the weeks in which he kept it in a mess. Praise the act of thoughtfulness and he may become more thoughtful and less inconsiderate. And when he fails, praise him for trying.

In all these ten rules for maturity in your relationship with your child, the key word continues to be *maturity*. You are helping your child to become a person who *becomes;* who is forever capable of changing, growing, and improving. And you are helping your child to become a person who, within the framework of his own powers, can do justice to the many and varied circumstances that fill his life.

The seed of the plant carries within it the core of maturity. How wonderful it is to watch the early stages of childhood as the seed sends forth a tiny root to hold it firm and a little green leaf to seek the sun! Then there is an entire root system to hold the developing entity secure against all winds. And more and more leaves, and strong branches, and then buds, and then flowers!

Chapter Nine

YOU
AND YOUR LIVELIHOOD

When he wrote *How to Live* about sixty years ago, Arnold Bennett said: ". . . it is true that success in its common acceptation is by its very essence impossible to the majority if there is an accompanying truth which adjusts the balance; to wit, that the majority do not desire success."

This seems a startling statment. Yet as one continues reading Bennett's thoughts, and the thoughts of many other profound thinkers, one comes to see that he states the basis of a great truth. Bennett continues:

> The average person certainly wants more money and the average person does not usually rest until he has gotten as much as is needed for the satisfaction of his instinctive needs. He will move the heaven and earth of his environment to earn sufficient money for marriage in the "station" to which he has been accustomed and precisely at that point his genuine desire for money will cease to be active. The average man flourishes and finds his ease in an atmosphere of peaceful routine.

The Talmud tells of a man who is beset by a bee. "Begone!" he says. "Give me neither your honey nor your sting." Most people go along with this reasoning. They settle for life on a moderate basis—just asking enough to satisfy their physical, emotional, mental and spiritual needs. Yet to satisfy one's needs requires living on a level considerably above poverty.

Let us follow along with Arnold Bennett:

> Men destined for success flourish and find their ease in an atmosphere of collision and disturbance. Naturally, the average man dreams vaguely upon occasion. . . . But to dream vaguely is not to desire. Often I tell myself that I would give anything to be the equal of Conquevalli, the juggler, or to be the captain of the largest Atlantic liner. But the reflective part of me tells me that my yearning to emulate these astonishing personages is not a genuine desire and that its realization would not increase my happiness.

Bennett concludes with an analysis of the average town of his day, a community of 20,000 to 30,000 people. He asserts that the few who take part in the struggle for success can easily be identified. Some have already left for distant pastures that seemed greener. Those who stay, by the time they reach their thirties, have begun to separate from the crowd. A dozen or so rule the town; they form the town council. Half a dozen others control the town's wealth and its commercial life. A few others, who teach science and art, are also reckoned among the distinguished.

What of the rest? Have they struggled for success and been beaten? Not they. As they grow old, do they resemble disappointed men? Not they. They, the majority, have gotten what they genuinely tried to get. They have never gone near the battle of success. But they have not failed, Bennett shows.

The average man who may question his maturity if he has not made a fortune should take heart. Bennett points out that the number of failures is surprisingly small. You see a shabby, aging man slip down the main street and someone says, "That's so-and-so, one of life's failures. Poor fellow!" The very tone in which the words are uttered proves the rarity of really failing.

Now, what Bennett tells us is that we all seek fulfillment—not necessarily success—in the satisfaction of work and the acquisition of money. Along these same lines, Emerson wrote in his essay on wealth:

> As soon as a stranger is introduced into any company, one of the first questions which all wish to have answered is how does

that man get his living? And with reason. He is no whole man until he knows how to earn a blameless livelihood. Every man is a consumer and ought to be a producer. He fails to make his place good in the world unless he not only pays his debt but also adds something to the common wealth. . . .

Emerson goes on to give due credit to wealth as a means of enjoying life, but, in other essays, he comes back to the golden mean, the averaging-out of life's compensations. What then is success? Bennett goes on to say:

One can no more explain success than one can explain Beethoven's C Minor Symphony. One may state what key it is written in and make expert reflections upon its form and catalogue, its themes, and relate it to symphonies that preceded and symphonies that followed it. In the end one is reduced to saying that the C Minor Symphony is beautiful—because it is. In the same manner, one is reduced to saying that the sole real difference between success and failure is that success suceeds.

For in the end, he intimates, "success" is a relative definition, a self-defined state. An ancient rabbinical dictum says, "Who is rich? He who rejoices in his portion." And so it is in the case of the average man. If he feels that success has been his portion in the acquisition of enough money, in a sufficient satisfaction from his work, then he is successful—no matter if we still prefer to see the epitome of success in the unusual driver, doer, and seeker.

We have seen that to seek money alone is a sign of immaturity. We know that money should be handled as a means, not an end; a symbol of the comforts and necessities and luxuries and experiences it can buy for you. So much being said, let us now say a word in praise of money.

Within the time of the last generation, too much has been said in condemnation of money. Too many sons and daughters point the finger of contempt at parents who have fashioned productive livelihoods. They see the older generation as engaging itself in purely materialistic, essentially nonproductive, and socially valueless money-grubbing.

Money, nevertheless, is our universally used and indispensable tool of civilization—no matter who runs the show. Business, equally despised by some, is the machinery that plans and creates what the common man desires. It is just as unrealistic to condemn the reasonable pursuit of money and involvement in business, as it is to ridicule the quest for God. God too is a name or a symbol for indispensable "things," the unplumbed forces and the slowly discovered mysteries of the universe. Even as we are unable to escape the immanence of God (or a Power beyond ourselves) so we never can escape the worldly yet inevitable meaning of money.

Some old concepts of God may be dead, but not the power we call God. Money can be called bad names, but money still goes on buying what is necessary. A farmer is said to have plaintively reflected: "They say that money is the root of all evil. Yeah? I sure would like to have some of that root." The New Testament refers to the *love* of money as the root of all evil—but still, we can appreciate the farmer's point.

Judaism taught long ago that without material substance and sustenance, man is unable to engage in spiritual quest or study. Christianity, despite its early emphasis on asceticism, recognizes the necessity of enduring support as the foundation of an enduring people. Personally, I never have seen a soul walking around without a body. A man may not be able to live on bread alone; but certainly, without bread, he cannot live at all.

No, there is nothing wrong with money! It is rather the ways in which men acquire money and the ways in which men use money that is often wrong.

Along these lines, let me tell you a humorous story that a very dear friend, a Protestant minister, told me. A wealth member of his congregation contributed $5,000 to a vital church rehabilitation program. A board member came to the minister and protested against his accepting the contribution. "How can you accept a gift from that man who derives his income from the running of gambling dens and houses of prostitution? It is unclean money." My minister friend replied, "Don't worry. When I get the money I'll clean it up before it's applied to church use."

This story implies that my friend would not condone the means

by which such a contributor acquired his money. He would, however, accept the fact that many a good cause is helped to stay alive
by money that comes from bad sources. The money is there, after
all. Why not use it to do some good?

Most of us earn money at some job or profession. For most of
us, repeated performance in that job or profession is necessary to
keep the money coming in. When is such work constructive to the
worker, and when is it drudgery?

In *What Men Live By*, Dr. Richard Cabot says,

> We work because we want the fruit of work, not from pure
> dogged determination. To force ourselves along without any
> desire for a goal of attainment is drudgery. Work is doing what
> you do not *now* enjoy for the sake of a future which you clearly
> see and desire. Drudgery is doing under strain what you don't
> now enjoy and having no end that you can now appreciate. To
> learn how to work is so to train our imaginations that we can
> feel the stimulus from distant futures as the coast cities of
> California get heat, light and power from distant mountain
> streams.

Work is not necessary only in order to make a living. Its primary
function lies in making a life. As Emerson says, every man is a
consumer and ought to be a producer. We can all call to mind the
names of men and women who possess more than enough money
to keep them in security, who do not work, and who are unhappy.
They sense they are only consumers, not producers; constant takers
and never givers. On the other hand, most of us know of wealthy
people who eagerly seek some interest or activity that demands
hard work, and will labor at it eagerly just for the sake of the joy it
gives them to be constructive. Again, most of us know men who
waited for the "great day" when they could retire from their jobs,
only to find that they could not endure the feeling of boredom
and uselessness.

Work gives a man a sense of worth in the eyes of his fellow men.
Slackers are uncomfortable in time of peace as well as in time of
war.

Work is excellent therapy. In hospitals for the mentally and
emotionally disturbed, a fundamental method of treatment is to

put the patient to work. I frequently urge bereaved husbands and wives to engage themselves in some absorbing work; to focus their thoughts and activities on matters outward from their grieving selves.

In work, we can often fulfill ourselves—not always, but often. The mature person stands the best chance of finding a means of livelihood that really interests him. And when that means of livelihood requires great dedication—such as the ministry, medicine, or law—the livelihood really chooses you. It calls you, and you cannot say no. Your friends may never understand why you choose to spend your days working so hard for less money than you could earn in other ways; but *you* know why. Yours is the maturity to make your peace with the losses for the sake of the deep, inner gains.

We shall now set down ten rules for the proper, mature use of money and the choice of work.

1. HOW MUCH MONEY DOES A MAN NEED?

In one of his finest essays, *How Much Land Does a Man Need*, Tolstoy tells of a Russian muzhik—a peasant—who learns that in a far distant state the authorities are giving away homesteads. As much land as a man can encircle by traveling around it for an entire day, from rising sun to setting sun!

The muzhik takes his family on a long journey to the distant land, and at break of dawn he begins to run, eager to encompass as much land as possible. In the intense heat of the sun he runs and runs without food or water. As the sun begins to set, he stumbles and staggers, but still he runs, heart pounding, and at length falls across the finish line—dead. Then Tolstoy brings home to us the fact that now the man is given all the land he needs: a plot about six feet by three feet, and no more.

Concerning money: you can*not* take it with you. Only the immature seem in a childish way to approximate "taking it with them" by spending many thousands of dollars on gaudy funerals and monuments and mausoleums of great cost.

During his life a man needs enough money to keep him in

decency and dignity, certainly above the poverty line of his day. He needs enough so that he can eat well, dress well, live in a comfortable and attractive home, enjoy some recreation, support his children on their way through college, give to good causes, and participate as a responsible citizen in community affairs. And at his death a man needs—not vast sums to leave his children—but enough to pay any debts he may have incurred and enough to take care of his burial.

It is no sin to have more; but it is only the immature person who cannot rest until he has more. It is then that the love of money can really become an evil, driving a man beyond his strength and badly affecting the family to whom he "gives everything."

Man must be master of his money, and not let money become his master. A mature man knows that the excellence of his work, the quality of his character, and his relationships with his own family and his neighbors measure him more validly than does the size of his bank account.

2. HOW SHALL A MAN ACQUIRE HIS MONEY?

Now and then I teasingly advise a young man in search of a bride, "If you meet a lovely, intelligent girl of fine family and excellent character, and she happens to be cursed with the possession of a million dollars, you still should not hesitate to propose to her if you love her. The money is her family's fault, not hers." By which I mean that inherited money is as valuable and serviceable as is earned money. What counts is what you do with the money.

It is immoral to acquire money by stealing, cheating, taking advantage of innocent people who trust you. And many of us shrink from acquiring money by playing the horses or through gambling of any sort. I do not think that gambling is immoral in itself—as some preachers contend—but gambling *is* destructive to one's self, often financially, more often psychologically. Also, I have seen many a friendship destroyed at a card game.

Even when a method of acquiring money is legal, it may be wrong. Even when the law is on your side, do not press your case too hard against a neighbor who may not be as powerful as you.

Read the "Laws of Holiness" in the nineteenth chapter of the Book of Leviticus, verses 1 to 18. Think on what this means: If you own a wheat field, you are entitled to all of its havest; but you *should* leave some wheat standing in a corner of the field for the poor to gather in. Today we have Courts of Equity to redress wrongs decreed by Courts of Law. Above all we have a higher moral law that cannot be enforced, but which a mature man nevertheless will obey.

3. HOW SHALL A MAN HANDLE HIS MONEY?

There are two extremes: the save-alls and the spend-alls; and there is the mature way of handling money that gives you far more in the end.

The ant and the grasshopper, whom we met some pages back, are prime examples of "save-all" and "spend-all" (at least, in the well-known fable). The ant, forever grubbing for food and living on very little while he painstakingly stored away all he could, was never able to enjoy the bright warm summer. The grasshopper did nothing but enjoy the fine weather and the flowers, but every year, when summer was gone, he faced the problem of starvation.

Human ants and grasshoppers are always with us. I recall a friend who lived beyond four score and ten. He lived comfortably but simply, gave generously and wisely but was cautious. When he died, he left an estate of over a million dollars. His wife had been carefully schooled in the art of saving, marketing, and cooking with the utmost frugality, even nursing her husband mostly by herself during his last long illness. She was much surprised by the size of the fortune her husband had left and she was dismayed at the thought of the increased enjoyment of life the money could have brought them. At least she can now make up somewhat for the many decades of "ant" living.

As for the grasshopper, everybody knows one. He spends every cent he has and lets tomorrow take care of itself. He is always in debt, does not really own his furniture or his late-model car; yet he pours presents into the hands of his friends and won't let anyone else pick up a dinner check. If he goes bankrupt, as is often the case, it is in a big way.

The mature man spends and also saves. He pays as he goes. He lets the Joneses live their way while he lives his. Both feet rest on the ground—one on the ground of the present, the other on the ground of the future, a future which never will catch him unprepared.

4. FOR WHAT SHALL A MAN USE HIS MONEY?

Some years ago, a civic-minded multimillionaire in a large community gave his daughter the most lavish and costly wedding those who attended had ever seen. There were some who criticized such extravagance. When I heard about it, I pointed out that this man was a very generous contributor to many charities and to his house of worship. I said that he who had shared so much of his wealth with others was entitled to spend all he wished on his loved ones, to make the wedding a rare family occasion and truly significant as the happiest day of his daughter's life.

The mature man gives his family first claim on his money. He knows his wife deserves an attractive home and attractive clothes. He helps his children to get the education they need as preparation for their lives ahead.

But even though a man and his own come first, his fellow man never should be far behind. Among the centuries-old traditions of the Jews is the tradition of charity. Even poor Jews who themselves are the objects of charity will often tack a tin charity box to the kitchen wall. Into that box go odd coins, which are collected for the poor of the town or for fellow Jews in need overseas.

The mature answer to the question "For what shall a man use his money?" is, "For the real good of himself and his family and at the same time for the good of others whom he may not know and who do not know him, but who are his brothers in mankind."

5. HOW SHALL A MAN SEE HIS MONEY?

A folk tale comes out of the European ghetto of the Old World. It tells of a man who was very wealthy but miserably stingy. He closed his ears against all appeals for help, whether it was for God's House or for charity.

Finally he was asked to come to the rabbi's study, where, after a long period of silence, the rabbi asked the rich miser to step to the window, look outside, and tell what he saw. Puzzled, the miser looked out and said, I see people walking up and down in the street." "Very well," said the rabbi. "Now look into my mirror and tell me what you see." The miser said, "Why, in the mirror I see myself." "Exactly," said the rabbi. "Through the glass of the window you see people. In the glass of the mirror you see only your own person. Do you know what makes the difference? It is the little bit of silver behind the mirror. Only when you do not look at silver are you capable of seeing others."

A mature man knows he did not acquire his money in a vacuum. His associates, his employees, those who taught him his business, the economy of his country and the world—all played their parts in putting money into his pocket. Thus, in a sense, he holds money only in stewardship for others. It is right that he spend on himself, but in seeing his money he should not see it locked into his private vault to be used for his own purposes alone.

It is mature to give what one can. For a rich man, it is all the more fitting to give generously. I once knew a rich man, however, who handed out large sums of money to many worthy causes, yet he did not really *give*. He used his money as a bribe to gain acceptance for his own will and his own way. There were thousands who had reason to be grateful to this man. There were few, however, who were his genuine admirers or friends. In his own way, he never looked away from his silver. And so though he looked at others, in them he saw only himself.

6. WHY YOU SHOULD BE EQUIPPED TO FOLLOW SOME LIVELIHOOD.

The ancient Jewish sages taught that every father is duty-bound to teach his son three things: Torah (God's law), swimming, and a trade. Knowledge of the divine law was to save the son from sin. Knowledge of swimming was to help him save his own life.

Knowledge of a trade was to save him from starvation, and to give him status, security, and self-respect.

Once again, we can consider the viewpoint of the person who is born into great wealth, or who early in life acquires so much money that it seems he never will need any more. Why should he not henceforth feel free to rise or lie down as he wishes, to go anywhere he will, to play, or to pursue the arts as the spirit may move him?

The mature man knows what the ancient sages knew; a knowledge of a means of livelihood provides not only money, but also status. There is a very essential respectability involved in being able to earn one's living and in knowing that one can contribute to society as well as take from it. I have noticed that many a wealthy man makes a kind of profession out of working for his church or for his community or his country. Many dollar-a-year men work harder than those who are gainfully employed. And again, the mature man knows that, unlike virtue, wealth can be lost through no fault of one's own. The wheel of fortune turns quickly. Businesses that are veritable gold mines today can become outdated tomorrow. Or riot, revolution, and oppression can make a fortune suddenly disappear.

We have seen many refugees from Nazi Germany come to these shores penniless—or nearly so. Many of them had special skills so that, in a few years, they were able to build new lives on the wreckage of the old. By the same token, we can see how many Negroes cannot take advantage of long-deferred rights and opportunities because of the lack of preparation.

Knowledge of a livelihood skill, a skill in demand at a business or professional level, is a great anchor in anyone's life. This seems obvious when we think of poor people. It applies to the rich as well, and of course to the millions in between.

7. WHAT LIVELIHOOD SHALL YOU CHOOSE?

One of my favorite tales is the following: An immigrant Jew landed in New York City and needed a job to keep him alive. In the Old World he had been sexton of a synagogue, so now he tried to find the same kind of work. But as soon as any congregation found out he could not read or write English, he was turned away.

He became a peddler. When he had a little money, he opened a little store. After a time he was running a very prosperous department store. One day he decided to build a needed addition to his business premises. He went to the bank for financing, and readily was offered a loan of $200,000. A note for the amount was presented for signature—and he made an X.

"You mean to tell me you can't write?" exclaimed the bank president in astonishment. "I can't read or write English," the prosperous merchant admitted. "Amazing! You are illiterate, and yet you are such an extraordinarily successful man. What might you not have achieved if you had been able to read and write!" "I'd have been sexton of a synagogue," came the ready reply.

The chances are that a man with such built-in talent for retail merchandising would have taken spare time from his sexton's duties to start a store. Built-in talent has a way of showing through. I have spoken of the way in which a calling will often choose its man, rather than the man choosing the calling, and this principle can be applied at many levels. I know successful businessmen who would have made superb clergymen. I know some clergymen who, after a few years, wisely left the ministry and became great successes in the business world.

No man is to be blamed if he has to "shop around" for a while before he finds the means of livelihood for which he is best suited. Often enough, one takes a job early in one's career as a matter of expediency; if your father or your uncle has a flourishing business and can make a place for you—why not? One of my own sons remarked, while in high school, that it would be much easier for him to find a job if I ran a business instead of a temple.

Where maturity comes into its own is in choosing a field when you have had time to sample a job or two—when you really know what you are doing. (I except those who know in their early years exactly what they want to do and be, and never falter.) It is maturity that guides you to give up a good job with your father-in-law because you don't want to be a puppet. Or to settle down to a long, hard grind of study when you are past the college years, because some profession at last has told you that, for you, this is it. However you go about it, be true to yourself in the way you earn your living.

8. SHALL YOU AVOID CERTAIN WAYS OF EARNING YOUR LIVING, EVEN THOUGH THEY BREAK NO LAW?

In the Talmud we find the story of a man who was upbraided for rejecting his son, who had become a wastrel. The unforgiving father is told, "You ought to condemn yourself, not your son. Remember, during his most impressionable years, you started him in business in a perfume shop in the Street of Harlots."

In every age, men have known that certain jobs, businesses and professions have an adverse effect upon those who engage in them. Or, as in medical and legal practices there is nothing basically wrong with the profession itself, but it does develop definite shady sides. Acting for the stage or screen seems to be that way too. The handling of other peoples' money, as the Rothschilds did it, was an honorable profession, and the Rothschilds proved that vast fortunes can be made under conditions of the strictest probity. Yet, for some, banking is a constant temptation to take crooked short cuts.

Beware of jobs that have any built-in tendency to strain one's scruples or to bring one down to a low standard of ethics or morality. Unfortunately, such jobs often return a good livelihood. The price is too high, however, when it amounts to selling one's soul in return for gold. The day of reckoning always comes.

The mature man sees his job as part of his constant changing and upward growth. He knows that no shoddy job can change him—except for the worse.

On the other hand, don't let prejudices and superstitions stop you from going into a job you like. For example, if you wish to become an undertaker—why not? The profession fulfills a valuable public service. Even as there are those who handle the circumstances of birth, so do we need those who take care of the circumstances and responsibilities that go with death.

9. MUST YOU LIKE YOUR MEANS OF LIVELIHOOD?

Some people say that if you do not like your job, you cannot do it well; or even that if you do not like your job, you aren't really living. Examine the word *like*, however, and you will find it too all-inclusive. I don't think there ever was anyone who liked all of his job all of the time. But a circumstance that causes the merest twinge of dislike to one can cause deep annoyance and bitterness in another. Maturity makes the difference. In helping you handle all the circumstances of your life, it helps you handle "dislike"—and to know a passing dislike from a permanent aversion.

A job first of all is a routine. A routine naturally will get in the way of something else we'd rather be doing on a fine day, for example. Thus often it is not one's particular job that becomes a target of dislike, but the very concept of *job*. Even when genuine dislike comes in, one must always balance it against various other factors. Is the job essentially worthy? Does it promise progress? Would the "bother" factor really not follow you if you went to another job?

Most of the affairs of our lives involve a long-term compromise with our likes and dislikes. In marriage most especially it is almost impossible not to have periods of grumbling; yet only the very immature will break a marriage because, now and then, dark clouds come into its sky. One hears a great deal of resentment expressed about the circumstances of marriage that "chain one down" with legal obligations, children to care for, and one's independence curbed. Yet many a job that was changed only transformed a passing annoyance into a long-term disaster; and the man who decided he had to like his job all the time, or else, ends up wishing there had been some stronger bar against changing.

This does not mean that one should remain chained to a job forever. If you are not happy in your job, change as soon as you can. But be as sure as possible about the new one before giving up the old one. Use your maturity as your guide, carefully but boldly. Looking into your three-way mirror, you see a man who needs a means of livelihood; who is better off if his means of livelihood is suited to his talents and his personality; but who also, being human, will never be entirely happy with any portion of his life. You don't have to like your job if it serves your economic need. Look well within yourself to make sure you know what "I don't like my job" really means.

Now and then a man is really "stuck" in a job. Realistically he sees that his stake is too high, or his chances elsewhere are too slim, or he has waited too long, and he simply had better stay where he is no matter how he dislikes it. Again, one's daily attendance at a certain job or profession can grow to be of such importance to others that one's own likes and dislikes are set aside. This is the case with many a clergyman, physician, businessman, lawyer, or a storekeeper. Once you make your peace with the fact that you must continue with your job, it is possible to do a much better job. Satisfactions can be found that were not seen before. Your maturity, helping you face up to life, finds compensating joys and treasures.

10. WHEN SHALL YOU BEGIN EARNING?

If you read *Oliver Twist* and similar works of the nineteenth century, you will appreciate what it meant for children to begin earning their living before the age of ten. The choice was often a brutal one; either they worked or they did not live. Frequently they were apprenticed in some trade and stayed with it for the rest of their lives. In many cases, that was good.

In our own America, even in the early twentieth century, children often had jobs that saddled them with long hours of hard work. The many Horatio Alger stories attest to this fact. The passage of child-labor laws—and the gradually lessened need for such labor—helped children to grow up healthier, better educated, and more fitted for life. The education explosion of our present space age makes it more and more necessary and possible for young men and women to continue their education at an age that would have seen them at work only twenty years ago.

Yet, there are thousands in high school and college who are merely marking time. College, especially, can be a four-year loaf. Such young people would be far happier and far more useful to society if they earned while they learned. They might take on a modern type of apprenticeship, free of the old semi-slavery. Apprenticeships can be keyed to the skills needed in trades; or they can be keyed to the more specialized needs of engineering, electronics, modern transportation, and so forth.

Learning need not stop when earning begins. The more the worker continues to enrich his mind and develop his talents, the more potential he finds in himself and the greater is his value to the community. When the U.S.S.R. was still in its infancy, exchanging butter for guns and playing Russian roulette with starvation, it invested heavily in developing the brain power of its youth. This has returned great dividends. The modern world needs more and more educated people——but we also must make sure that education does not waste itself in ivory towers. The world is built on work. Let us never downgrade work or money. They are the basic soil in which a rich and vital civilization flourishes and flowers.

Chapter Ten

YOU
AND YOUR HAPPINESS

Many of us know the story of *Mutiny on the Bounty,* or have seen it in either of its two motion picture versions. Who can forget Charles Laughton's commanding voice bellowing, "Mr. Christian!" and adding to the injustices that set up the mutiny—led by Clark Gable.

There really was a mutiny on a real ship named *Bounty.* The cause of the mutiny seems to have been the inhumane actions of Captain Bligh; but, between the lines, one can see other factors. Surely one of them was the feeling among the mistreated English sailors that they could find a permanent haven on some beautiful island like Tahiti, where they had been able to stay for an enchanted while. There, in a balmy climate of sunny days and moonlit nights, living at the bounteous breast of nature, they could end their days amid a happy native people, without wants or cares.

As it turned out, the mutineers dared not stay at Tahiti, where other English ships might call. Most of them ended their days on Pitcairn Island, regretting their isolation, and finding life not so easy as they had thought it would be. Yet had they stayed on Tahiti, had they never been molested, would they have been happy? The almost certain answer is *No.*

When you try to escape the world, you can leave behind the gray skies of the northern regions, the responsibilities of your job, your debts, and everyone who ever bothered you, but you take along yourself. What is a civilized man who has escaped to a tropic island? He is someone whose general temperament and thoughts, basic emotions and ambitions, fundamental desires and fears remain the same. He may find he is happy. In that case, however, he is a man who is quite capable of being happy anywhere because he is happy with himself. Basically, happiness depends upon what you are as a person, not upon the place where you live.

As someone put it very well: If Jesus goes in through the door, it is Jesus who will come out. If Judas goes in through the door, it is Judas who will come out.

When Joe E. Brown was starring in the play *Harvey*, I asked him to tell me the line in the script that he liked the most. He knew it instantly—a line said by Harvey's slap-happy friend: "I always have a wonderful time wherever I am and with whomever I am."

Joe E. was one of those people who know that a man makes his own happiness. He does not have to let his happiness depend on where he is or upon the people around him. His happiness depends, rather, upon his own approach to that place and those people.

Nor will he find it necessarily in the possession or enjoyment of things. I have seen many times that when a man becomes too heavily tied to material matters, he finds it difficult to evoke happy relations with other people. "Uneasy lies the head that wears a crown," for the crown and all its responsibilities and dangers must ever weigh more than the simple pleasures of life. There are many kinds of crowns. Only the other day I lunched with a man of great power in the business world and possessed of enormous fortune. He is on intimate terms with scores of men like himself. None of them, he told me, is happy. He went on to examine the general reason for the millionaires' unhappiness, and I was not surprised to find that it hinged on very personal matters. As a rule, these men seemed to have faulty relationships with their wives and children. Their money had pushed them into a way of life that gave them such faulty relationships—and nothing money could buy could mend the damage that had been done.

It does not follow that money must bring misery, or that poverty

—or having just enough money—brings happiness. Nor does it follow that the inevitable truth is the other way around. Happiness always is a personal matter. A truly mature rich man will never let his money sour his life. A truly mature poor or middle-income man is entirely capable of being happy. Ultimately, your life is what *you* yourself make it.

The world's literature and folklore are full of stories that point out how futile it can be to *seek* happiness. Rather, happiness is a blessing that comes to you as you go along; a treasure that you incidentally find.

Maeterlinck's *The Bluebird* tells such a story. A woodcutter's boy and girl, Tyltyl and Mytyl, keep a blackbird in a cage in their home. What they want, however, is the bluebird of happiness. They set forth from their humble hut to find this fabulous bluebird. Since the story is a fantasy, it has the seekers wandering through many lands, even the lands of those who have died and those yet to be born. Eventually they return disappointed and discouraged—only to find that happiness is next door. Their blackbird, lent to a neighbor's sick child, turns gradually into a bluebird. At last the children realize that the bluebird of happiness was always at home.

Russell Conwell was noted for the lecture *Acres of Diamonds* which he gave thousands of times over a period of some years. It tells of a man who heard that in a faraway place he might discover a rich diamond mine. Leaving his home and his loved ones, he journeys through many lands and suffers many hardships, but finds no diamond mine. Old and starved, he dies, still searching. Meanwhile another man has taken over his home. The new owner sees on the fireplace mantle an unusual rock the size of an egg that the former owner had picked up on his property one day and had placed there as a curiosity. Examining the rock, he notices how it shines when he rubs away the dirt. It turns out to be a remarkable diamond. Digging in the back yard, the new owner finds more diamonds. The man who had died in such misery and want had never thought to look for a diamond mine in his own back yard. And so—the lecture goes—few of us ever help ourselves to the riches of all kinds that wait within our reach. We need only open our arms and gather them in. This includes the riches of happiness.

Often, a man is convinced he will be happy when he attains a certain goal. Sometimes he is. Often he is not, for one way to avoid being happy is to set conditions on happiness, to say, "Thus I am able to be happy" and "Thus I am not."

You often can see this phenomenon at work among mothers. First they will say, "When Johnny gets out of elementary school, I'll be happy!" And they are for a while. Next you hear them telling their friends, "When Johnny graduates from high school, I'll be so happy!" And they are, at least for the summer. Johnny's graduation from college brings the same result, and so does Johnny's marriage, and so does the birth of Johnny's first child, when Momma becomes an ecstatic grandmother and the feeling may continue until she becomes a baby-sitter. If Momma has not learned how to be happy in between her special blessings, she does not know much about being happy.

Serendipity, a word coined by Horace Walpole, is defined as accidentally finding unexpected things while working on something else. So it often is with happiness. Some people go through life seeking it but never seeing it. Others, engaged in the faithful performance of their daily tasks, or in doing good for their fellow men, find they are also consistently happy.

Once again, as we did earlier in this volume, let us make the point that happiness is not to be confused with pleasure. Pleasure might be a very gratifying sex experience; but if it were gained as part of a deceitful adulterous relationship, unhappiness waits to move in. One may gain a stunning triumph—some great goal gained after years of trying—but if the winning of the goal leaves scars of physical and emotional damage, no real happiness is attained. Happiness runs deep; it is an undercurrent of life. Pleasure is transient, mere pretty bubbles that rise to the surface and can be briefly admired before they break.

Contentment is perhaps closer to happiness, yet it is really something else. I am thinking of an old story called *Bontsche the Silent.* Bontsche, from the day of his birth till the day of his death, was the victim of every kind of misfortune. He knew poverty and misery, rejection and persecution. But he never complained. (My own note on the story: Noncomplaining is not always a virtue. It may show only lack of awareness as to what is possible to one in life.) When he died, and appeared before the Heavenly Throne for judgment, a Divine Voice called out that his sojourn on earth had been most exemplary in its saintliness, and that as a reward he might have anything his heart desired. Bontsche hesitated, wondered, finally stammered forth, "Might I please have a buttered roll for breakfast every morning?" So underprivileged had he been that this had become his ultimate idea of happiness.

Happiness should be relevant to you. You should be conscious of your capacity for happiness, and never consider yourself as one "doomed to sorrow" or never-ending depression.

In your further understanding of happiness, however, know that there is animal happiness and human happiness. Animal happiness is essentially physical and human happiness is primarily mental and emotional. How can you bring happiness to a dog or a cat or a horse? You make sure it has adequate food, comfortable quarters, affectionate attention, and freedom to roam and romp. In short, an animal is made happy by the same factors that make a human child happy.

The surest sign of immaturity in a human being is his contentment with animal happiness. In children, we expect it. We know they are primarily interested in having fun, in stuffing themselves with goodies; in *getting*. Only as maturity begins to arrive does the child show evidence of feelings that are not completely selfish, and that encompass also the joy of giving. Now he can sow the seeds of deep, mature happiness. He need not at any time in his life deny his interest in physical pleasures, although he will observe some sense of balance. He will, however, give a higher degree of the cerebral to his concept of happiness, and so he will find he is more deeply and maturely happy.

Now we shall set down some definite criteria of happiness. You will note again that so many factors that many people regard as being essential for happiness are more closely related to passing pleasure. But nothing can be defined in a completely all black-and-white, pattern. We begin with five criteria that seem very desirable, and yet are not the essence of genuine happiness.

1. LIFE

Of course, without life, you would not be able to be happy. At the same time just to be alive is not sufficient reason for happiness. The ancient Hebrew toast, "To life!" is not intended to refer only to the counting of one's years. It refers rather to making one's years count. It is a toast to life lived on a plane far higher than the animal.

The ancient sages had a way of speaking that can be puzzling to the uninitiated. Know the true meaning of some of their sayings, however, and you know you are face to face with truth. Thus, they asked, "How shall a man live?" "Die," was the answer. This meant that a man was to slay all that was ugly and mean in himself, and so live truly and worthily.

They asked, too, "How shall a man die?" The answer was, "Live." This meant that if you live in a self-centered, animal-like way, concerned only with your own pleasures, without any thought for real happiness, and you will effectively slay all that is worthwhile.

Remember Oscar Wilde's *The Picture of Dorian Gray*. In addition to dealing with a magical picture, it drew a word picture of a man who destroyed himself by the way he lived. His idea of happiness was to fill his life with the satisfaction of all his animal urges; to eat and drink like a glutton; to gratify his sexual passion wherever and whenever possible; to fill each day with the largest possible amount of play and the least possible work.

Thus did Dorian Gray destroy himself. The saddest part of this story is that it is largely autobiographical. Oscar Wilde, despite his great talent, never knew mature happiness. In *De Profundis*, written while he was in Reading Gaol, he set down this line to his friend, Lord Douglas: "It was only in the mire we met." Wilde at length saw what he had done to himself by wallowing in mire. It was too late then for him to gain a spiritual mountaintop where the ground is firm and the air is pure and the view is always broad and far and clear.

To have life, then, is to have the opportunity to find true happiness. To say that one is happy merely because one is alive is to beg a vital question.

2. SUCCESS

I began my book *The Road to Successful Living* with these words:

> The most conspicuous failure in our time is success. No age in man's history has been so feverishly occupied with success; no age has been so noisily boastful of it. The reality or the promise of "good things" pervades our view of the world; almost everywhere plenty has replaced or has begun to replace poverty.

But I went on to point out that this same age of ours has beheld:

> . . . one of humanity's recurrent disillusionments, one of the great unlearned lessons of history. Success does not create happiness. . . . For half a century it has been taught by both precept and example that material success—distinction in the acquisition of fame and money, position and power—is the most important goal in life. . . . Material success is what a man has; spiritual success is what he is; and we had tended to lump them together, to assume that happiness was the product of weath. We had been proved wrong.

We spoke earlier in this chapter of the kind of mother who keeps on making conditions for happiness, tying those conditions to the life-progress of her son. The son, himself, if he acquired his mother's point of view, would have trouble in proving to himself that he ever was happy and not just waiting for happiness. Being in the lower grades, he would dream only of high-school-level happiness. Discovering that high-school studies made demands upon him, he would yearn only for college, a golden dream. Finding out that college life involves something more than song fests and football games, he would yearn for the happiness of having a job. Once he had a job. . . . But you can see the sequence here.

Let us go back to the question of goals. It is easier to set up a specific goal, such as making a million dollars or becoming president of a large corporation, than a general goal such as missing no opportunity to help one's fellow men. I know a man who thought he would be happy if he accumulated $100,000 by the time he was forty. He had his hundred thousand before he was forty, and set his goal at a higher level. Reaching it, he wanted a million; he got his million dollars—and wanted more. Was he happy? He could not rest; he wanted more, more, and *more*. He was another of those men who came to wonder dismally why he could not master so simple a skill as getting along with his wife and his children.

Was Alexander the Great ever happy? While we may remember his conquests, we remember him most as the man who died at thirty-three, unhappy because he had no more worlds to conquer. Was Napoleon ever happy? He wanted power and he acquired power; but never enough. There *never* is enough. And he died frustrated, exiled, and lonely.

Thus, much hinges on one's definition of *success*. In that sense, the person who knows deep, mature happiness has succeeded in life. Set aside, however, all ordinary definitions of success when you relate it to happiness.

3. SECURITY

What kind of security do we mean here? Again we must take *security* in its meaning for most people; financial security.

Who has it? We must first rule out the millions who fall asleep every night—if they can sleep—with one last worried thought as to whether they will be able to pay their bills, meet the rent, count on holding their jobs long enough to pay off on the refrigerator . . . and every other thought that goes with chronically not having enough money.

You would assume that those who do have a good supply of money must feel secure! Alas, they do not. To the immature, "financial security" is so relative a term that it hardly can be said to exist. Many of my readers will be able to recall the wave of suicides that ran through Wall Street at the time of the great crash in 1929. The record showed later that many a man who jumped out of his office window was neither penniless nor anywhere near penniless. But to be reduced from a multimillionaire to the ownership of only a few hundred thousand dollars is more than some men can tolerate.

Nor does a rich man have to lose his money in order to show how little it does for him by way of giving him true, inner security. It is not too uncommon for a man with millions to keep his wife on a miserly allowance. A noted multimillionaire—he *succeeded* in making a certain soft drink popular all over the world—would approach hysteria every time he had to write a check to pay his taxes.

I have heard it said, "You either have security or you don't have it." This is true when we talk of the only real security, inner security. Yet those who have it not can seek it and often find it— once they know that security is not measured in money, nor in friendships, nor in anything else that can fade away.

4. PASSIONATE LOVE

The ancient teachers looked upon our Sacred Scriptures as being primarily concerned with spiritual love, the love of man for God, the love of man for man as his brother.

What then are we to make of The Song of Songs? Here is a paean in praise of young, physical love, telling—though in delicate and muted terms—of female charms and sexual urges. How did this somewhat profane book find its way into the Biblical Canon? Among other explanations (rather far-fetched), scholars have said that after all it was designed to teach us the meaning of real, mature love. They center their interpretation upon the following lines:

> For love is as strong as death. . . .
> Many waters cannot quench love.

Passionate, youthful love, then, can eventually become mature, deep love. Love can be carried far past youth, and, on its own better terms, last all one's life despite the ravages of time and circumstance. Love can become a maturity; a strength with which to meet all circumstances.

Passionate love has its place. To deny the passions of youth would be to deny human nature. Only remember that this kind of love—to many, the only kind of love—has no firm connection with happiness.

Unfortunately, passionate love is more dramatic than mature love—more visible, more amenable to treatment in song and story. The hit parade is always top-heavy with songs of love at a romantic, if not passionate, level. Love stories last through the ages. Thwarted young love will be a theme for the novelist and poet forever.

Passionate love can be a great wellspring of pleasure. It also can be a source of considerable torture, whether the loving two discover they are different people after all, or the fatal third party enters. The mature person may enjoy passionate love, yet he knows it is passing. And he knows that any passing phenomenon is no fit foundation for happiness. Mature young people can love each other deeply, yet their essential happiness is a factor that strives beyond their passion.

Within a family, there may be deep love and yet constant bickering. I know many children who love their parents but somehow must quarrel with them. Surely this love brings no happiness to either side.

5. PEACE

Joshua Loth Liebman's Peace of Mind was published over twenty years ago. Peace still remains as individual a matter as it did in his portrayal. Certainly there is no general peace, either within or without. Despite our great strides on various fronts of material progress, we are still torn by inner tensions and live now with special terrors, knowing that one false move can depopulate the earth.

With all this, we must realize that there cannot be any such condition as absolute peace on earth—except the peace of the tomb. Again I quote from my book *The Road to Successful Living:*

> The peace of life cannot be perfect and it cannot be permanent. The very essence of living is movement, and movement always encounters resistance. And resistance means conflict. Armed warfare may some day cease—and soon, we hope: but the inner conflicts of humanity will never be totally resolved. Peace on earth in the political sense is a distinct possibility—even a necessity—but absolute personal peace of mind for all men everywhere is millenial and a dangerous illusion at that.

The mature man knows that only someone who lives like a vegetable, bereft of the vital processes of thinking, feeling, and aspiring, can ever have peace of mind. But that does not mean that an active man cannot have happiness. Some of the most genuinely happy men and women I know are involved in associations and activities that trouble their days and disturb their nights. In giving of themselves to others, in working eagerly without pay for worthy causes, however unpleasant that work may be, they find a happiness unknown to those who seek only peace.

So long as our minds are active, our hearts sensitive, and our souls searching, we always shall be occupied in refashioning our environment according to our heart's desire. Discontent need not take away our happiness. There is great wisdom in the words *divine discontent.*

We have examined five vital values that many will say are basic to human happiness. We have seen that—in their general conception at any rate—these values are not really the essence of happiness.

What then are the permanent values that do make for happiness? I shall now set them down in a positive program for the attainment of happiness. They are a sense of being, a sense of belonging, a sense of meaning, a sense of growing, and a sense of giving. We may call them the five spiritual senses that correspond to the five well-known physical senses of seeing, hearing, smelling, tasting, and feeling. The physical senses give us great capabilities for pleasure. The spiritual senses can guide us to true happiness.

1. A SENSE OF BEING

In his *The Importance of Living*, Lin Yutang reminds us that the three great religions of China, Confucianism, Taoism, and Buddhism, shared in common a very common-sense earthy approach to the pursuit of happiness. Consequently the mature Chinese was a person who never allowed himself to become so immersed in thought that he drowned out all his emotion or to become so completely wrapped up in any one idea or ideal or philosophy or faith that he failed to appreciate his own entire being—the joy of just being alive. Merely *to be*—to wake up in the morning; to behold the glory and grandeur of this world; to satisfy a healthy appetite; to experience the normal functioning of the body; to talk with friends; to look upon the face of loved ones— that is happiness enough. The mature Chinese, in contrast to his Occidental brother, gives his emotions and instincts much freer reign; he is less subject to inhibitions and restrictions. Like the character in the musical who sings, "I enjoy being a girl," he enjoys just being a man. *To be* is a great privilege even if you are incapable of great thought or great achievement. Read the Bible, particularly some of the Psalms and The Song of Songs and you will find the same approach to life and love.

As anyone who reads Lin Yutang's book will recognize, he is too profound to be opposed to the use of the intellect. He tells us, rather, that our Western world has placed so much emphasis on thinking that it has downgraded feeling. He is not asking man to give up the cerebral processes that make him human, but only to enjoy himself at the same time on a level of *being*, where he can be happy with what he is.

I asked a very brilliant nun of the Catholic Church what happiness is. After some careful thought, she answered in essence, "We are all so restless that we fail to rest; to look inward more than outward; to let our eyes rest on nature as well as man." She went on, "To be happy you must have a sense of being, always knowing you are part of a wonderful world, reflecting upon the joy of your being, physically, mentally, emotionally; meditating upon the mystery of the universe, marveling at the magic of nature and of human nature."

I know people who have developed the art of solitude. When others are trying hard to "find something to do" in leisure hours, these people find happiness in sitting alone in a park to admire the trees and listen to the birds; or in taking long walks, luxuriating in the sun and the wind. This is far more than merely being alive. It is a full tasting of the essence of life; of *being*. It is a communion with one's inner strength and at the same time a "tuning in" of one's own self to forces beyond and above. *Being* is the overall experience, the very foundation of a happy life.

2. A SENSE OF BELONGING

A generation ago, Eugene O'Neill gave us his play *The Hairy Ape*. In it he portrayed a hairy-chested ape-like stoker named Yank, who shoveled coal in the boiler room of a transatlantic liner.

I shall attempt in my own words only to approximate Yank's way of speaking. He demands of his fellow stokers: "What's them slobs in the first cabin got to do with us? We're better men than they are, ain't we? Sure! One of us guys could clean up that whole mob with one mitt. Put one of them down here for one watch in the stokehole. What'd happen? They'd carry him off on a stretcher. Them boids don't amount to nothin'. They're just baggage. Who makes dis old tub run? Ain't it us guys? Well den, we belong, don't we? We belong and they don't. Dat's all."

One day, Yank, curious, wanders into the first-class passenger section in the upper part of the ship. Accidentally, he comes face to face with a beautiful, aristocratic, well-bred girl. Startled and shocked by his big, brawny, hairy-chested, hulking figure and vacuous face, she shrinks back with obvious revulsion and rejection. She shows the kind of fear that one might feel if one were to meet a ferocious hairy ape in a forest.

This is a very painful experience for Yank. Slowly he tries to think his way through it. It tells him in no uncertain terms that he does not really *belong*; he does not really belong to the human race.

In the last scene we find Yank in a zoo, talking through the bars of a cage to a gorilla inside. Says Yank to the real hairy ape, "You're lucky. See? You don't belong wit' 'em and you know it. But me—I belong wit' 'em but I don't, see? They don't belong wit' me. That's what." Yank opens the cage and says to the gorilla, "Step out and shake hands!! I'll take yuh for a walk down Fift' Avenue. We'll knock 'em offn the earth and croak wit' the band playin'. Come on, brother" The gorilla grabs Yank in its enormous arms and crushes him to death. Dying, Yank gasps, "I'm t'rough. Even him don't think I belong." And then the final, despairing cry, so typical of so many lost people, "Christ, where do I get off at? Where do I fit in?"

Man is a gregarious animal, and gregarious in more than the physical sense. Not only does he wish to mingle with others; he also wants to mingle his thoughts with the thoughts of others, to work with others in attaining common aspirations, and to be accepted as a worthy member of human groups such as the family and the community. As regards these groups, we also increase our sense of belonging by joining ourselves to others; we become members of a particular religion, citizens of a particular nation. Most of all, we belong to our fellow men and they belong to us in our sharing of membership in humanity; we are concerned with each other, and that basic concern comes through despite quarrels and misunderstandings.

Yank, a great muscular child, found his belonging only at one level, in the companionship of the stokehold. Most of us find the sense of belonging at many levels. Yet few of us can stand up against a rejection that leaves us without orientation, as though we had been robbed of any place to stand in the world. This may happen to a child when he begins his conscious life without a feeling of love around him. He may never quite be able to get over that basic disorientation.

Even those who most value the highly individual sense of *being* know that in joining themselves to others they fit themselves all the

better for the enjoyment of life. Belonging is ever a part of happiness, and maturity thrives in one who knows how to share his
world; how to belong.

3. A SENSE OF MEANING

To feel one's meaning in the world is closely akin to belonging.
More particularly, we connect meaning with purpose and worthy
achievement.

Thus, a man is helped to feel he has meaning when his job has
meaning. Richard Cabot published a list of seven requirements
for a good job, of which the last four are particularly significant:

4. A chance to achieve, to build something, and to recognize what we have done.
5. A title and a place which is ours.
6. Connection with some institution or some firm or some
   cause which we can loyally serve.
7. Honorable and pleasant relations with our comrades at
   work.

He goes on to say that we all like "to believe that our intentions,
our hopes, our plans, our daily food and drink have not passed
through us for nothing, for we have funded their worth in some
tangible achievement that outlasts them. . . We need something to show for ourselves, something to prove that our dreams
are not impotent."

A wife needs to know that her job of household work has great
meaning for her family. A child needs to know that he has meaning in his parents' life, and he can be permanently hurt if he is
made to feel he is just another mouth to feed, just another nui-
sance that cannot be avoided. A person whom we help should now
and then be given a chance to help us in some manner, so that
he feels the meaning of the *giving* side of life.

In *To Let*, one of the several volumes of *The Forsyte Saga*, John
Galsworthy portrays two aging servants whose only work is the
care of a very ancient Forsyte. This special job becomes their
special pride. In my own experience, I have seen a cook or a maid

who has spent years half-helping, half-annoying a family with her lax, lazy work, suddenly change into an eager, conscientious worker when the family became really dependent upon her.

The meaning of a life may be held so firmly as to transcend life itself. One of the best-known lines from the speeches of the late Martin Luther King is, "If a man doesn't have something worth dying for, he isn't fit to live." Not all will find the happiness of meaning at that transcendent level. Yet all of us can find the meaning of involving ourselves with mankind in matters beyond our daily jobs.

4. A SENSE OF GROWING

One of the greatest misfortunes in human life is to be retarded in growth. This is particularly true of physical retardation because it is always visible. I have been close to the agony of boys and girls who through some defect are doomed never to grow beyond four feet in height—and must be told. And I have watched them develop a mature approach to their plight, put aside self-pity, and become the happiest individuals in a circle of young friends. They even develop a sense of humor about their affliction. They turn a liability into an asset. Maturely, they grow within.

One of the happiest communities I have ever come across was in a school for the mentally and emotionally retarded. Some of the happiest parents I have met have been the mothers and fathers of retarded children. It is true that some retarded children are happy because they are incapable of feeling the trials and tensions that make for unhappiness, yet even with the retarded, the sense of growing is a sense of happiness. Learning the use of a few new words, realizing that one has made a friend, or developing —after many trials—some small but useful skill are meaningful and delightful growth to these children. It is also the basis of usefulness, of belonging, of meaning. To see their retarded children grow just a little is one of the greatest joys of their parents.

In our time, intellectual growth has become the "in" thing. Acceleration and expansion of learning for normal children now begin in their nursery years. An increasing number of adult classes in many fields is another sign of the educational thrust forward.

To increase our emotional growth, however, still remains a problem difficult to solve. In the midst of a world filled so heavily with injustice and cruelty, hatred and violence, how is one to grow in charity, compassion, mercy, forgiveness, and love? The development of this emotional (and spiritual) growth is the goal of all great religions. It is basic to the growth of maturity, which, as we know, is in itself a constant inward growth.

5. A SENSE OF GIVING

Just what is giving? In the physical sense, it usually amounts to handing over part of one's excess possessions to someone else—usually someone in need. This can be a mechanical motion. As we saw previously, money can do good no matter where it comes from and no matter in what spirit it is given. True giving includes a gift from within. It must be a gift of the heart along with the gift of the hand. Money may be its outward and necessary symbol, but one who really gives knows how to give part of himself.

Anyone who takes part in the management of charity drives knows there are ways in which to get increased donations. In a large city, the Community Chest's board of directors found that a certain prominent and prosperous merchant had donated only $500 to the annual drive. They called on the man.

"Mr. X," they said, "we know you are one of the finest and fairest men in our city. Isn't it part of your responsibility, along with the rest of us, to take care of the indigent, the blind, the aged, and the orphaned?"

"Yes," said Mr. X. "It's not that I don't believe in supporting charitable agencies. But I'm sorry, I am simply not a charitable man. I know others in my position give more, but I give what I give and that's all there is to it."

The directors smiled. Their spokesman said, "We ourselves once felt that way, and we had to learn. Let us help you learn how to become charitable. You will find there is a great happiness in giving. Now, we thought a man like you would give, say, $15,000. Never mind that. Why don't you just make out a check for $5,000 to the Chest, this year, as a beginning. Next year I know you'll want to give more."

Confronted with the sense of *noblesse oblige*, presented with an image of himself that he felt impelled to live up to, the merchant wrote out a check for $5,000. The next year, he gave more. In a few years he became one of the city's biggest and proudest givers. Or, was he truly a *giver*? As his fellow citizens watched, they came to appreciate having his money but somehow they never could appreciate him. They felt he never learned to give himself with his gift. Giving made him proud, gave him status, but never really made him happy.

That strangely gifted, strangely troubled man, Oscar Wilde, wrote a fable, *The Happy Prince*, that begins:

"High above the city on a tall column stood the statue of the Happy Prince. He was gilded all over with thin leaves of fine gold; for eyes he had two sapphires, and a large red ruby glowed on his sword hilt."

There came a swallow who had delayed his winter trip to Egypt and on his hurried way happened to put up for the night between the feet of the statue. The swallow discovered that the Prince was weeping; he wept at the sight of the poverty and misery of the poor people in his city. The swallow was persuaded to stay long enough—too long into the winter—to help the Prince give literally of himself as he distributed riches to the poor. First the swallow took the ruby to a mother tending a sick child so that his health could be restored. Then the swallow carried one sapphire eye to a starving writer in a cold attic. The other sapphire eye was flown to a little match girl. Then, one by one, the swallow carried all the leaves of gold that covered the Prince's body to give aid to under-nourished, emaciated children.

Now the Prince had given himself away. In the cold of the winter, his leaden heart cracked. So too did the swallow die in the cold.

" 'Bring me the two most precious things in the city,' said God to one of his angels, and the angel brought him the leaden heart and the dead bird."

Long ago it was said, "It is more blessed to give than to receive." One who has not learned how to give can learn; and perhaps he will learn more easily if he does not have excess money. Or if he lacks any money to give, he truly gives himself—in attention, in service, and in time taken from mere pleasures and so transformed into happiness because it is time used for *giving*.

Thoreau once said that most men lead lives of quiet desperation. This probably is an exaggerated statement, but it is certainly worth remembering and using as a measure against one's own state of mind.

At best, most of us make a compromise with contentment. We have pleasures, and from time to time we feel real joy. But also we experience many misfortunes. Sometimes all we can see and feel is the sorrow that rains upon us. And so we may conclude that happiness is only a will-o'-the-wisp, an empty dream. It is not to be found in the here and now. Perhaps it is waiting in the sweet bye and bye.

For that reason, most religions provide the concept of an afterlife. With it may come the vision of a Messiah who will at length deliver mankind from its vale of tears.

The concept is comforting. As with the concept of God, there is no way of proving or disproving it. I trust we have learned, however, that real, deep-down happiness *is* attainable in this life, on this earth. Every chapter of this book reveals that happiness is bound up with every value of maturity; and that every value of maturity helps us to be happy. Happiness need not be considered as a permanent, unflawed state, but rather exists as a bedrock foundation of living, sensed and felt and trusted no matter what storms may arrive.

You can find maturity. You can find happiness. You can find maturity and happiness no matter who you are or where you live or what your age may be. Maturity and happiness are always close by. In fact, you carry the seeds within yourself right now.

Chapter Eleven

FINDING YOUR
MATURITY QUOTIENT

And now our book is almost finished. But its subject—the quest for maturity—will never be complete. Like maturity itself, a state of *becoming*, it never can be complete.

We have come far, however. I hope your insight into maturity—and into your own maturity—is broader and deeper and better illumined than it had previously been. Keep on watching and checking your maturity. Regularly examine the ten pillars of maturity in your house of life; do not allow them to crack and crumble. View yourself daily in the three-way mirror with its forty maxims and check the figure of your personality.

Those who are married will do well to consult the ten special guides to maturity in marriage at least once a week. Those who are also parents should extend their review through the section of ten on children. Whoever you are and whatever your niche in life, you would do well to concentrate on the twenty points made in Chapters Nine and Ten. These are major guides along the road to wise, happy, and mature living.

Many people become fond of their own faults. One can excuse one's self so easily by asserting, "Well, that's the way I am and that's all there is to it." Or you'll hear someone say, "I'm sorry I have such a poor memory," and there the matter ends; he never will do anything about improving his memory, or adjusting whatever other lack may be hampering him.

It is not so much a matter of being against self-improvement as it is of being against *change*. Maturity is a *becoming*—therefore a changing—and, therefore a progression toward the better.

Think of the Weight Watchers. Having found themselves beset by ugly, unwanted, hampering, unhealthful fat, at length they take themselves in hand and *change*. Their slogan is: *I love myself more than I love food*. And they *watch* to make sure they are changing in the direction they want to go. Mounting the scales every morning, counting calories, pushing themselves away from a temptingly loaded table, they gradually get the results they desire. They improve their appearance, they become lighter, more active, and more comfortable. They improve their life expectancy. And what's more, they greatly improve their self-respect—their enjoyment of themselves as persons who refuse to become the victims of their weaknesses.

So too can you be a Maturity Watcher. Join the Maturity Watchers today! Most of us are too "fat" in immaturities. Say firmly, say repeatedly: *I love myself more than I love my immaturities*. Watch—and act. A dozen times a day you may find you are handling some situation in a way that could be improved—slanted toward maturity. Soon the more mature handling of life-situations becomes a habit. And this of course is the other index of maturity; the better and more capable and wiser handling of the circumstances of life.

It is often apparent that a person is more mature than his neighbor; that A is immature for his years or B is very mature for a young person and will certainly become even more mature as he grows both in years and experience. But how is one to measure maturity?

Along these lines, I have noticed that educators and psychologists can establish one's intelligence quotient—one's I.Q. Physicians also can advise you about your physical or body quotient—call it the B.Q. Neither I.Q. nor B.Q. can be established very exactly; and now we move toward a new measurement that is even less exact—maturity quotient or M.Q. Yet the M.Q. is valuable as an indication of one's general level of maturity, general direction of maturity, and general (and important) maturity potential.

You are ready to measure your own M.Q. By now, you know it

is no vague generalization; that your maturity is strongly bound up with your success as a human being and your success and happiness in your career, in love, in achievement, and in all of life. To measure your own M.Q., take a pencil and sit down with this book in some quiet place. Check off Yes or No on the list of 101 immaturities that follows. These immaturities are stated as questions. Asked honestly of yourself, each question leads you to an honest Yes or No answer.

Inevitably, as you go along, the questions will remind you of people you know well. Your husband or wife or child or friend or neighbor or boss or co-worker will appear before you, labeled with a characteristic immaturity. There is nothing strange about this. Were *they* to go through the same list, the chances are very good that they would recognize *you*.

Concentrate, however, on seeing yourself. Taking the 101 questions one at a time, it is as though you unrolled a long tape measure against your own person. Be frank. This is your book, and you are finding your own maturity quotient. If you care to copy off the questions and keep them (and your Yes-or-No checkmarks) with your own private papers, do so. But do not neglect any question. Ask it of yourself and demand of yourself a Yes or a No.

You will find the questions arranged in five major categories, beginning with immaturities that can be overcome with comparatively little effort, and going on to those whose defeat may require heroic measures. I repeat: answer each question with a Yes or a No. Answer each question before you read the next one. Answer every question, question by question, no matter how insignificant or irrelevant some question may appear to you.

When you have finished, you will have a complete score sheet and will be able to calculate your M.Q. With certain discounts and allowances for the quality of one's basic maturity core and the particular stage of one's life, this Quotient will be fairly accurate for each age period. Your first answer need not be your final answer, however. When you have finished the 101 questions, go back to the first and check through one by one. Study your answers. You may change a few, on second thought.

Above all, do not resist saying Yes because it may hurt. The hurt can be nothing but your resistance to knowing yourself. As with the Weight Watcher who trains himself to refuse second helpings —think of the benefit and you can forget the hurt.

Now you are ready to find your M.Q. Take your pencil and begin.

MATURITY QUOTIENT ANALYSIS

Category A

	YES	NO
1. Do you often say: "I just can't stop smoking"?	___	___
2. Do you often say: "I just can't cut down on eating"?	___	___
3. Do you often say: "I can't stop drinking hard liquor"?	___	___
4. Do you frequently give the excuse: "Sorry, I'm too busy"?	___	___
5. Do you find yourself frequently apologizing: "Sorry I'm late"?	___	___
6. Do you often apologetically say: "I have such a poor memory"?	___	___
7. Do you often say: "Sorry I'm so stupid, but I don't understand"?	___	___
8. Do you constantly excuse yourself with: "Sorry I'm such a poor correspondent"?	___	___
9. Do you often say: "Sorry, I'm just not sociable"?	___	___
10. Do you excuse yourself with: "If only I had more time"?	___	___
11. Do you assert positively: "I'll never do it"?	___	___
12. Do you dodge with: "I don't know"?	___	___
13. Do you hedge with: "I guess so"?	___	___
14. Do you insist: "I believe in fate"?	___	___
15. Do you sigh: "I can't make any friends"?	___	___
16. Do you usually wait for someone else to introduce himself first?	___	___

YES   NO

17. Do you self-righteously proclaim: "I can't be a hypocrite"?   ____ ____

18. Do you confidently proclaim: "I'm not interested in money"?   ____ ____

19. Do you get out of helping causes by saying: "I just can't ask people for money"?   ____ ____

20. Do you feel that you can always do things better than anyone else?   ____ ____

Category B

YES   NO

1. Do you often excuse yourself with: "I intended to do it"?   ____ ____

2. Do you frequently dodge with: "I'll try to do it"?   ____ ____

3. Are you a compulsive talker?   ____ ____

4. Are you a poor listener?   ____ ____

5. Are you a chronic complainer?   ____ ____

6. Do you frequently apologize with: "I'm just too tired"?   ____ ____

7. Do you excuse yourself with: "I'm just not good with my hands"?   ____ ____

8. Do you shy away with: "I just can't speak in public"?   ____ ____

9. Do you excuse yourself with: "I just can't help it"?   ____ ____

10. Do you frequently dodge with: "I know I just can't do it"?   ____ ____

11. Do you regretfully exclaim: "If only I could get started"?   ____ ____

12. Do you often say: "I'm sorry, I just can't handle money"?   ____ ____

13. Are you usually impatient?   ____ ____

14. Do you judge others on the basis of rumors?   ____ ____

15. Do you positively assert: "I can't forgive"?   ____ ____

YES   NO

16. Must you be constantly entertained?   ____ ____
17. Do you stubbornly say: "I've always been this
    way and I can't change"?   ____ ____
18. Must you usually be the center of attrac-
    tion?   ____ ____
19. Do you dodge decisions with: "Well, I'm not
    sure"?   ____ ____
20. Are you resentful when someone doesn't re-
    member you?   ____ ____

Category C

YES   NO

1. Do you frequently stop a discussion with: "I
   know what I'm talking about"?   ____ ____
2. Do you consistently try to tell other people
   what to do?   ____ ____
3. Do you think that material gifts can create
   strong friendships?   ____ ____
4. If you don't like a person, do you refuse to
   deal with him?   ____ ____
5. Is it hard for you to admit you are wrong?   ____ ____
6. Is it difficult for you to apologize?   ____ ____
7. Do you get upset easily by discourtesies?   ____ ____
8. Do you get angry quickly?   ____ ____
9. Do you frequently say: "People are not
   friendly"?   ____ ____
10. Do you excuse yourself with: "If only I had
    listened to my father and mother"?   ____ ____
11. Do you excuse yourself with: "If only I had
    had a good education"?   ____ ____
12. Do you excuse yourself with: "If only I had
    gone into a different business (or profes-
    sion)"?   ____ ____
13. Do you excuse yourself with: "If only I had
    married someone else"?   ____ ____

YES   NO

14. Do you excuse yourself with: "If only I had
    remained single"?   ___ ___
15. Do you excuse yourself with: "If only I had
    been born beautiful (or handsome)"?   ___ ___
16. Do you excuse yourself with: "If only my
    parents had been wealthy"?   ___ ___
17. Do you excuse yourself with: "If only I had
    not had such a bad environment when I was
    young"?   ___ ___
18. Do you excuse yourself with: "My trouble is, I
    was an only child"?   ___ ___
19. Do you excuse yourself with: "If only my
    home had been full of love"?   ___ ___
20. Must you always have the last word?   ___ ___

Category D

YES   NO

1. Do you expect people always to be nice to
   you?   ___ ___
2. Do you expect never to be rebuffed or rejected?   ___ ___
3. Do you stoutly assert: "I don't need anyone's
   help"?   ___ ___
4. Do you frequently say: "It was my idea," or
   "If it hadn't been for me"?   ___ ___
5. Do you find it hard to take criticism?   ___ ___
6. Do you frequently get into arguments?   ___ ___
7. Are you easily hurt?   ___ ___
8. Do you expect everyone to love you?   ___ ___
9. Is it hard for you to admit failure?   ___ ___
10. Is it difficult for you to take advice grace-
    fully?   ___ ___
11. Are you unable to keep friends for a long
    time?   ___ ___
12. Do you always expect gratitude?   ___ ___

YES   NO

13. Do you inordinately crave publicity?   ____ ____
14. Do you snub people regularly?   ____ ____
15. Do you habitually say: "I am certain it is so"?   ____ ____
16. Do you generally blame others instead of yourself?   ____ ____
17. Do you excuse yourself with: "If only I had had his opportunities"?   ____ ____
18. Do you complain: "I lost my job because they didn't like me"?   ____ ____
19. Do you explain: "They don't like me because they are jealous of me"?   ____ ____
20. Are you in the habit of saying: "I know I can't do it"?   ____ ____

Category E

YES   NO

1. Must you always be top dog?   ____ ____
2. Must you always win?   ____ ____
3. Must you have everything you want?   ____ ____
4. Do you expect life always to be simple and smooth?   ____ ____
5. Do you worry because you worry?   ____ ____
6. Are you unable to close doors on things that are gone forever?   ____ ____
7. Is it difficult for you to admit you've made a mistake?   ____ ____
8. Have you a drive for perfection?   ____ ____
9. Must you always be happy?   ____ ____
10. Do you generally cry over spilt milk?   ____ ____
11. Must you always be right?   ____ ____
12. Do you constantly insist on having your rights?   ____ ____
13. Must you always have your way?   ____ ____
14. Does someone else's success trouble you?   ____ ____
15. Do you act out of envy or jealousy?   ____ ____

                                                        YES   NO

16. Do you hesitate to sacrifice for a meaningful
    objective?   ____ ____
17. Does sorrow continually nest in your hair?   ____ ____
18. Do you feed on grudges and hatreds?   ____ ____
19. Do you brood over disappointments and
    defeats?   ____ ____
20. Is it difficult for you to trust anyone?   ____ ____

The 101st Immaturity Bonus

                                                        YES   NO

Do you disagree disagreeably?   ____ ____

That is the end of the questionnaire. As for the bonus: If the
answer will be helpful to your score, substitute your *No* for a
harmful *Yes* anywhere among the other 100 questions. Your score
will be based only on the first 100 questions.

Before you score yourself, read the following instructions:

There are differences of value in some categories. Category A
is worth 10 points; each "A" answer is worth ½ point. Category
B is worth 20 points; each "B" answer is worth 1 point. Category
C is worth 40 points; each "C" answer is worth 2 points.
Category D is worth 20 points; each "D" answer is worth 1 point.
Category E is worth 10 points; each "E" answer is worth ½ point.

Don't forget to give yourself an extra favorable answer, anywhere, if your answer to the Bonus Question was favorable. For
every *No*, credit yourself with the number of points indicated—
anywhere from ½ to 2, depending on the category. Take no credit
for any *Yes*. As you probably noticed, the highest grading value
is assigned to Category C because it points to personal traits that
definitely stand in the way of one's personal welfare, success,
peace of mind, and happiness. Category A, on the other hand,
contains immaturities with which most people can live without
suffering serious consequences. Category E contains immaturities
that are part of your natural life style; they are harder to overcome. Since the cost to you is already great in the possession of

these immaturities, the penalty here is lighter. Category B contains immaturities that are not too serious though they do make life a little difficult. Category D contains immaturities which are fairly serious but can probably be overcome.

Now total your score. Remember, you give yourself the rating for each answer in each category only if your answer was *No*. If your answer was *Yes*, score nothing. When you have totaled each category, add the totals together. Your grand total is your M.Q.— your Maturity Quotient.

Before considering the significance of your score, let us once again set down the several stages of life we discussed in Chapter One:

1. infancy
2. from 7 to 14
3. from 14 to 21
4. from 21 to 40
5. from 40 to 60
6. from 60 to 75
7. 75 onward

Now we can consider your score—at first only in a general, non-related way. A grade of 75 or more is *super*; 65 is *excellent*: 55 is *good*, 45 is *fair*; 35 is *poor*; 25 is *bad*.

Let us relate these scores to the stages of life. Only in the sixth and seventh stages of life—after the age of 60—are you likely to rate *super*. Although it takes more than experience to bring full maturity, only in our later years are we likely to have enough experience with all the vital factors of maturity to make our maturity rich enough and full enough. If you score 75 in an earlier stage of life (and it's an honest score based on deep thought) then truly your maturity is *super-super*.

A grade of 65—excellent—is possible at the third stage and even at the second stage of life, as early as age 14. But keep in mind that a grade of 55 (*good*) at stages two and three is worth as much as a grade of 75 at stages six and seven. Age is not necessary for maturity. Still, the more years you live, the greater is your opportunity to develop your maturity core.

Sometimes a person knows he cannot score himself honestly. In such a case you may ask your husband or wife, a trusted friend or close associate to score you, or to give his or her opinion as to your own scoring. Then your score may become higher. If it becomes lower, don't worry. Better to see yourself clearly than to wear blinders. To know yourself puts you a great step ahead.

When you do know your M.Q.—and it's a great window that lights your inner being—put your maturity to work! Read this book again. And again. Let your M.Q. score and each question, carefully considered, serve as a crowbar to pry you loose from immaturities of thought and speech and behavior.

You can stop smoking when your voice of maturity, long stifled or ignored, now reminds you: *Do I love smoking more than I love being healthy and living longer?*

You can change your eating pattern in content and calories, letting your maturity give you the benefit of the long, hard-won experience of others in nutrition and weight control. And by the same token, when your maturity backs up your will, *you can* give up hard drinking, or give up drinking altogether.

You can learn, for example, that you learn when you listen. You can observe that anger is rarely worthwhile and is often damaging—and, maturely, you can profit by your observation. You can get used to the idea that not everybody is going to like you; for if that were not so, you'd have to be a very strange sort of person indeed. You can maturely realize that people will be ungrateful, unkind, inconsiderate—and yet you can live with them, for where are you going to find perfection? You can find happiness in maturity—within yourself—rather than a false and strained pseudo-happiness that requires your being forever in the spotlight, having everyone admire you (although they may laugh at you behind your back). You can be happy without being a millionaire, and you maturely know that high office and powerful position are no guarantees of happiness.

As a mature person who uses his maturity, who works every day to perfect and strengthen the great life-lever of his maturity, you know you can't be happy all the time. You also know you are going to be wrong sometimes; and have been wrong in the past;

and can expect to suffer as well from other peoples' mistakes. With maturity, you meet these circumstances; you learn; you go on, always stronger, always better, always *becoming*. And with maturity you find the great happiness of not wanting everything—as a child wants everything that glitters—yet of knowing what you really want. And now you have resources of mature judgment to guide you in attaining love, enough material possessions, a good mixture of pleasure and true happiness, and all else that makes life great and good.

As a supreme example of a man whose maturity was constantly becoming until the day he died, I once again call your attention to Pope John XXIII. Read his *Journal of a Soul* carefully and you will find the story of a man who used his daily confessional as a three-way mirror in which he might see and study his immaturities. At an early age, he discovered that, like all of us, he had a tendency to become angry, to be petty, to be jealous, to be resentful, to be overly ambitious and filled with false pride. He resolved to conquer these immaturities; not to submit to them. So he constantly checked and rechecked and corrected them until he became one of the most mature personalities of our time. He was a life-long Maturity-Watcher. The *Journal* reveals a human being who developed a constant sense of joy in life and in living; a sense of belonging to all humanity and all humanity belonging to him; a sense of meaning in every one of his actions and activities; a sense of constant growing; and a sense of continuous giving. He changed himself and changed the world. As a result when he left us in his eighties, he was universally admired, honored, and loved.

You may construct your own kind of confessional and create your own type of journal. Follow his example and you will find your maturity always becoming. Be a Maturity-Watcher.

Much more could be written on this boundless topic. Should this book prove itself useful and helpful, perhaps a sequel will follow, probing wider, extending higher into areas we have already explored and into others left untouched.